TALES OF THE EARTH

TALES OF THE EARTH

NATIVE NORTH AMERICAN CREATION MYTHOLOGY

DAVID LEEMING

REAKTION BOOKS

In memory of Little Antelope and Jake Page

Published by Reaktion Books Ltd
Unit 32, Waterside
44–48 Wharf Road
London N1 7UX, UK
www.reaktionbooks.co.uk

First published 2021
Copyright © David Leeming 2021

Printed and bound in India by Replika Press Pvt. Ltd

A catalogue record for this book is available from the British Library

ISBN 978 1 78914 499 4

CONTENTS

Preface

The myths of a people are their cultural dreams. In this book my purpose as a non-Native American is to study these dreams with a goal of better understanding the people who lived in what is now the United States before my ancestors' arrival.

To treat the mythology of the native North Americans as a viable category is, of course, intellectually dangerous. The more than five hundred tribes in North America all have their own mythological traditions. These tribes are part of early migrations to the Western hemisphere that included the ancestors of the indigenous peoples of Meso-America and South America. An obvious universal presence in Native North American mythology, however, is the creation myth. Scholars have long noted the existence of several basic creation myth types in world mythology. These include types that are amply represented in Native North American mythology: the *ex nihilo* (from nothing) creation, the from chaos creation, the world parent creation, the earth diver creation and the emergence creation. What stands out in Native North American creation myths of all types is the animistic concept of the spirit-infused sacredness of the land and everything in it.

I have begun with an introduction that provides a context for the mythology. Where did the first Americans come from and how and why did they come? How were the first Americans seen by the

Ernest Smith, *Sky Woman*, 1936, oil on canvas. The painting depicts a moment in the Haudenosaunee (Iroquois) narrative of the world's creation in which a woman falls from the Sky World toward the dark watery world below.

Europeans who 'discovered' America later? What is their role or lack of a role in the identity the United States has attempted to establish for itself? Each chapter that follows the introduction is concerned with a character who plays a significant role in Native American creation myths. Chapter One treats the figure usually translated as 'the Great Spirit'. The myths focusing on the Great Spirit are generally *ex nihilo* and from chaos creations. Chapter Two studies the ubiquitous but ambivalent character known throughout the world as the trickster. In Native North America the trickster – Coyote, Raven, Iktome and many other incarnations – is both highly creative and destructive. He aids the Great Spirit or the Goddess in creation, sometimes even becoming the culture hero who teaches the people how to use creation, but he instigates elements such as death that, at least seemingly, undermine that creation. Chapter Three considers the central role of the goddess in many Native American cultures (especially matrilineal ones) and their creation myths. The subject of Chapter Four is the hero. In Native American mythology this hero is sometimes specifically a culture hero, or his quest is to slay the monsters who threaten creation. A conclusion addresses the position of Native American mythology in the values and priorities of the United States. What is the place of Native American mythology in historical and modern American culture? How does Native American earth-based polytheistic mythology coexist or conflict with European American monotheistic and nationalistic mythology?

Native American mythology has, until relatively recently, been passed down orally rather than in written form. Versions of myths vary not only from tribe to tribe but from village to village, clan to clan, family to family, storyteller to storyteller, and medicine person to medicine person. There is no Native American equivalent of the Bible, the Quran or the Vedas. Native American mythology is an oral mythology. Myths were written down by non-Native Americans such as Henry Schoolcraft, George Bird Grinnell, Jeremiah Curtin,

Lewis Spence and Hartley Burr Alexander, and indigenous people such as Jesse Cornplanter, beginning only in the nineteenth century, and by later scholars and collectors, including Richard Erdoes, Alfonso Ortiz, John Bierhorst and N. Scott Momaday, to mention only a few. The retellings in this book are based on combinations of these and many other sources, including conversations with Native Americans.

Jean Leon Gerome
Ferris, *The First
Thanksgiving,
1621, c.* 1912,
oil on canvas.

Who Are the Native Americans?

Every American schoolchild knows that Christopher Columbus 'discovered' America in 1492 (or maybe it was the Viking Leif Erikson in the eleventh century). The same children are told that in 1620 English Puritans, referred to as the Pilgrims, came to America on the *Mayflower*, and that in 1621 they celebrated a thanksgiving harvest feast with people (including a native named Squanto) who already lived there. They are told, too, that Columbus, when he had arrived in what we still call the West Indies islands, believed he had found his way to India, and so he named the inhabitants 'Indians'. This is a name that has ever since been attached to the inhabitants of the Americas who were there when Europeans arrived. Children also learn that other English people – not Puritans – had arrived in America even earlier than the Pilgrims and had settled Jamestown, Virginia, in 1607 under the partial leadership of Captain John Smith. Smith was captured by Native Americans who already lived in Virginia, and it is said that he was saved from execution by the brave intervention of an Indian princess, Pocahontas.

Elements of these stories are apocryphal. But the essential truth about all of them is that when Europeans – whether Leif Erikson, Columbus, John Smith, the Pilgrims or earlier explorers in the early seventeenth century – arrived, the Americas were already populated by well-established nations of people. These people included

D B: Bouttats fec. Antverp

Æ tatis suæ 21. Aᵒ 1616.

Maloaks als Rebecka daughter to the mighty Prince Powhatan Emperour of Attanoughkomouck als Virginia converted and baptized in the Christian faith, and Wife to the worᵗ Mʳ Tho: Rolff.

Unknown artist, after Simon van de Passe, *Pocahontas [in Europe]*, after 1616, oil on canvas.

those discovered by the Spanish in the southern and western regions of North America, discoveries that preceded those of the English. Florida was occupied by the Spanish under Pedro Menéndez de Avilés in 1565 following initial raids by Hernando de Soto. What is now New Mexico was explored by Francisco Vásquez de Coronado before Juan de Oñate created settlements there in 1598. The most obviously advanced of the Native American nations prior to European invasion existed further south in Meso-America (modern-day Mexico and Central America) and South America. When the Spanish conquistador Hernando Cortés arrived in the Aztec capital

Opposite:
Pieter Balthazar Bouttats, after Theodor de Bry, 'Admiral Christopher Columbus Discovers the Island of Hispaniola', engraving from Antonio de Herrera y Tordesillas, *Historia general de las Indias Ocidentales* (1728).

13

View of the Avenue of the Dead and the Pyramid of the Sun, from the Pyramid of the Moon in Teotihuacan, Mexico, *c.* AD 100.

View of the ancient
Incan buildings of
Machu Picchu, Peru,
15th century.

of Tenochtitlan in 1519 he found a city larger and much better appointed than any European city. And much older cities had existed in Meso-America and South America before Tenochtitlan.

Much the same could be said of the huge Incan empire in what is now Peru when Francisco Pizarro conquered it in 1533.

The civilizations of North America were less dazzling to the Europeans than were those of Meso- and South America. But the native peoples associated with the stories of the English and Spanish settlers of what are now Massachusetts, Virginia and New Mexico were themselves anything but primitive by European standards of the time. In fact, across what is now the United States, long before the arrival of Columbus, there were thriving nations. These nations did what societies in other parts of the world did. They traded, fought wars against each other and dealt with the problems of communication arising from many languages; they raised crops, hunted, worshipped and domesticated animals, and some built impressive cities marked by monumental structures. Patuxet, the Wampanoag Indian village that would be taken over by the Pilgrims as Plymouth, was one of many well-developed agricultural and fishing settlements along the Massachusetts coast. Further west at the confluence of the Mississippi and Missouri rivers were the great pyramid-like mounds of the indigenous city Cahokia that were built at least as early as the twelfth century. Still further west were the spectacular cliff dwellings of the pre-Pueblo (Anasazi) peoples, complex living places abandoned for riverside villages (pueblos) in the thirteenth century, two centuries before Columbus's arrival in the West Indies.

Several initial questions arise naturally in connection with the indigenous population of pre-Columbian America. Who were these people? Where did they come from? When did they first arrive in the Western hemisphere? What was the effect on them of the Europeans who arrived after 1490?

Towards the end of the twentieth century an archeological consensus placed humans – often referred to as 'Paleo-Indians' – in

the Western hemisphere beginning perhaps as early as 16,500 years ago. It was generally assumed that these people came to America from Central Asia by way of Beringia, a wide land bridge (in some places as wide as 1,600 kilometres (1,000 mi.)) between Siberia and Alaska. The land was exposed some 25,000 years ago before being covered by the rising Bering Sea some 10,500 years later and then by a shallow frozen sea for another 10,000 years.

It was believed that over the centuries some of the Paleo-Indians, after gradually crossing Beringia, made their way south in pursuit of

Cliff Palace at Mesa Verde National Park in Colorado, *c.* AD 600.

game by way of an ice-free corridor between receding glaciers, some proceeding down into Meso-America and South America, some moving gradually into the North American Southwest, the Plains, the woodlands and the east coast. For many years the so-called Clovis people, named for a site dating back some 13,500 years near Clovis, New Mexico, were thought to be the earliest Americans.

More recently that consensus has been challenged by several individual archeological and anthropological studies that have concluded that humans lived in the Americas much earlier. Digs in southern Chile and Brazil, for instance, have uncovered artefacts at least 30,000 years old, meaning that the migration took place

Peopling of America through Beringia.

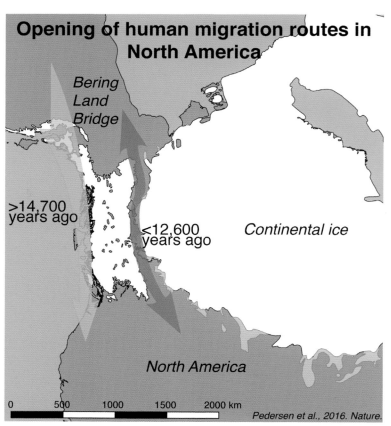

Opening of human migration routes in North America

Bering Land Bridge

>14,700 years ago

<12,600 years ago

Continental ice

North America

0   500   1000   1500   2000 km

Pedersen et al., 2016. Nature.

long before there was a glacier-free corridor, and perhaps even before Beringia existed. Various theories have developed around this migration, one being that some Paleo-Indians followed the Pacific Coast south in boats. In short, however, all answers to the origins and the routes of the first Americans are still undergoing research and may never be known. For many indigenous people in North America today, their ancestors originated in America, emerging from the earth or from the sky in ways suggested by creation myths told by each native group. However and whenever they came to America, the Native Americans thrived there in one way or another for thousands of years until they and their lands were 'discovered' by Europeans.

In what is now the United States, Native Americans were everywhere. In the Northeast were the Iroquoian speakers and some Algonquian speakers. The Iroquoians included the Iroquois Confederation and the Wyandot (Huron) group. The Algonquians were the Lenape (Delaware), Menominee, Pequot, the Wampanoags of the Pilgrim Thanksgiving fame, the Algonquins, Cree, and the Ojibwe of what is now the Great Lakes region and southeastern Canada and many others. In the Southeast were the Cherokee, the Chickasaw, the Creek and the Seminole, all four of which were descendants of an older culture known as the Mississippian. In the Plains to the west were many tribes, including the Arapaho, the Cheyenne, the Comanche, the Crow, the Dakota or Lakota (Sioux), the Kiowa, the Osage, the Pawnee, and the Siksika (Blackfoot). South of the Plains, in what we now think of as the American Southwest, were the Ute, the Paiute and, still further south, the Pueblo peoples along the Rio Grande River and its tributaries, the Zuni and the Hopi further west, and the late arriving Athabascans, the Apache and the Dine (Navajo). Still further south were the desert people, the Akimel O'odham (Pima) and Tohono O'odham (Papago) of present-day Arizona. In the Northwest Plateau east of the coast were the Nez Perce, the Okanagan and others. On the northeast coast were the Haida, the Tlingit, the Tsimshian and several others. In what is now California were the Chumash, the Maidu, the Modoc, the Ohlone, the Yokuts and their many neighbours, now mostly extinct or greatly diminished in size.

The most startling result of the 'discovery' of America was the effect it apparently had on the indigenous population that was already there. Estimates of that population in 1492 vary greatly. Some guesses range as high as 18 million, some as low as 1 million (a much larger population existed in Meso- and South America). By the beginning of the twentieth century the Native American population in the United States stood at about 250,000.

One anthropologist, Henry F. Dobyns, who specialized in Native America, estimated that in the first 130 years of contact between these tribal nations and Europeans in the Western Hemisphere, 95 per cent of the indigenous people died, mostly from epidemics of smallpox and other European diseases to which they had never previously been exposed. The Wampanoags of the first Thanksgiving story had already been decimated by contact with European explorers, who, beginning in the 1520s, introduced them to a plague-like disease, attacked them and sold many into slavery. In 1616 a European ship had arrived in their land with smallpox on board, so that by the time of the *Mayflower* four years later, the Wampanoags were in no condition to resist the Europeans successfully.

The population figures are still debated. In any case, the Native American population in the United States today stands at about 2 million across some five hundred tribes or nations. A quarter of Native Americans live on reservations. From the indigenous point of view, those who question the larger estimates of the original population do so to undermine the horrendous cost to the indigenous people of the European invasions. Lenore Stiffarm, an ethnologist of Nakoda and Kamai ancestry, told Charles Mann, as reported in his book *1491*, 'You always hear white people trying to minimize the size of the aboriginal populations their ancestors

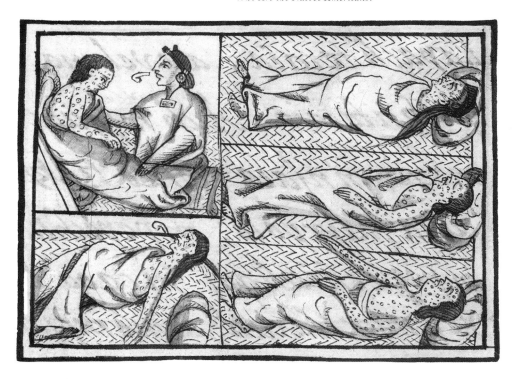

personally displaced . . . it's perfectly acceptable to move into unoccupied land . . . And land with only a few "savages" is the next best thing.'

The term 'savage' is one that was once commonly applied to Native Americans, either in the romantic sense of 'noble savage' or simply in the sense of inferior, uncivilized and dangerous. In both senses the 'savages' stood in the way of the newcomers and challenged what the Europeans saw as their own racial, religious and cultural superiority. For the Pilgrims of New England, Squanto and his people could teach useful agricultural lessons – how to fertilize their plantings with fish, for example – but to the Europeans what was important was that the indigenous peoples were not Christian, and that they seemed to resent the Pilgrim presence in what was rightfully their homeland. In 1675 the Pilgrims of Massachusetts

Illustration of the victims of a smallpox outbreak in 1520, from Fray Bernardino de Sahagún, *Historia general de las cosas de nueva España: The Florentine Codex*, vol. XII (1577).

23

Detail from Benjamin West's heroic, neoclassical history painting *The Death of General Wolfe*, depicting an idealized Native American, 1770, oil on canvas.

defeated what was left of the Thanksgiving tribe in battle and sold hundreds of its members into slavery. For the settlers of Jamestown, the Native Americans were dangerous barbarians who needed to be either subjugated or, like the noble savage Pocahontas, 'civilized' after being displayed as a curiosity in Europe. The Spanish conquistadors, by contrast, saw *their* Indians as a source of gold and as candidates for conversion from uncivilized pagans to semi-enslaved Catholics.

What the invaders and the settlers who followed them did not do, as they gradually appropriated more and more indigenous land, was to attempt to understand or learn from the people whose land they were taking. Instead, what the invaders and settlers saw as native obstructionism, something to be eliminated violently if necessary, was accompanied by a purposeful ignorance of Native American history and significance. This deliberate ignorance has persisted into our day, fuelled by a combination of guilt and embarrassment. To move beyond such ignorance and away from the scholarly arguments of non-Native Americans about Native American identity, it seems reasonable to turn to Native Americans themselves, especially to their myths. As cultural dreams, myths are a rich source for the understanding of a culture, and the obvious place to begin is with creation myths, those which reveal a cultural sense of collective self and collective priorities. Several basic creation myth types are represented in Native America. The most common type involves a supreme being's creation of the world from nothing (*ex nihilo*) or from a chaotic state or material. The second is the so-called 'world parent' creation in which the world emerges from a relationship between a Sky Father and Earth Mother or from the sacrifice of one of the parents. The third type is the 'earth diver' creation, usually involving a mother goddess and several animals who retrieve the elements of earth from the depths of primeval maternal waters. The fourth type, prevalent in the American Southwest, is the 'emergence' creation, in which the people are 'born' from Mother Earth.

In almost all Native American creation myths the sacredness of the land itself is emphasized. Four character types stand out in the myths. The first is a supreme creator deity sometimes translated as 'the Great Spirit'. The Great Spirit is often represented on earth by a culture hero, a being who teaches the people how to live, how to to create, how to feed themselves and how to arrange their societies. This figure is sometimes a trickster, an amoral but highly creative shapeshifter who can undermine creation by introducing such elements as pain, conflict and death. The third, and arguably the most important, figure is the goddess, who takes many forms but who is always directly associated with the sacredness of earth itself. The fourth character is the hero, the one closest to the human psyche in its quest to overcome the monsters that plague us.

ONE

The Great Spirit

In world mythology the dominant creation myth type is the
ex nihilo creation in which the world is born in the mind,
the words or the acts of an omnipotent deity. In the biblical
book of Genesis, God decides to give form to the void. In one of
the creation myths of ancient Egypt the creator instigates the life
process with his own semen or saliva. The creator may also work
from a form of chaos or undifferentiated material such as primordial waters, clay, a cosmic egg or simply darkness. In Hesiod's Greek
creation myth, the goddess Gaia (Earth) springs out of the primeval void called Chaos. In the mythology of the African Dogon
tribe the world is formed from the material contained in cosmic
eggs, and in a Babylonian myth the fresh waters of Apsu join with
the saltwaters of Tiamat to give birth to land.

In Native American mythology the supreme being, the 'Great
Spirit', is omnipresent but often not anthropomorphic, and not
extensively mythologized. More like the Vedantic Hindu concept
of Brahman – the creative principle behind all reality, existing everywhere and yet nowhere – than the monotheistic personal God of
the Bible and the Quran or the high gods of Greek and Egyptian
myths, the Great Spirit is an ineffable source behind an animistic world in which everything is a spiritual vehicle. Various Native
American Great Spirit figures such as the Algonquian and Plains
Indian Gitche Manitou or the Iroquois Orenda may reasonably

McKee Springs
petroglyph, possibly
a Great Spirit figure,
c. 1000, Dinosaur
National Monument,
Utah.

be said to be essentially a single concept, one central to animism wherever it is practised. Whatever metaphorical form he is given, the Great Spirit is the life energy within all living things. The Oglala Sioux medicine man Black Elk conveys this sense of the Great Spirit, known to his tribe as the Wakan Tanka. To Black Elk the Wakan Tanka was the 'center of the universe', a centre that is 'everywhere', even 'within each of us'.

The Great Spirit, then, is the cosmic energy that powers the universe. It is this element that leads inevitably, especially under the influence of the European invaders and their personal God, to the convenient relationship between the Christian God concept and that of the Native American Great Spirit. Where the two concepts coincide most easily is in the idea of a supreme being as creator. Even when the Native American creator is given anthropomorphic form, however, he interacts only slightly, if at all, with humans. He remains a distant figure, more a concept than an actual being. The Indian activist Russell Means preferred to refer to the Great

Spirit as the 'Great Mystery' to clarify the difference between the anthropomorphic biblical supreme being and the Native American ineffable spiritual essence of all life.

There are, of course, examples of the Great Spirit as a more anthropomorphic creator. Rather than theological vehicles – stories to be literally believed – however, these myths appear to be metaphors, in some cases even humorous ones, that make the abstract concept of the Great Spirit more accessible.

Some of the Ute people of southwestern Colorado and Utah say the creator was Manitou, a Great 'He-She' Spirit who lived in the sky, alone except for the sun, clouds and rain, among other natural wonders. A time came when Manitou found that it wanted something different. Maybe He-She was lonely. Whatever the reason, Manitou dug a hole in the sky and looked down into what was a vast emptiness. To do something with the emptiness, Manitou poured rain and snow into the hole and then some of the dirt that

Tichnor Bothers, *Smile of the Great Spirit, Lake Winnipesaukee*, c. 1940, colour postcard.

Smile of the Great Spirit, Lake Winnipesaukee, N. H. from Mt. Belknap

Black Elk and Elk
of the Oglala Sioux
as grass dancers,
touring with
Buffalo Bill's
Wild West Show
in London, 1887.

had been excavated by the digging. The dirt formed some plains
and a mountain, which He-She stepped down onto. He-She looked
around and saw that this mountain and others, as well as the sur-
rounding plains, could be improved by trees, grasses and other
plants. So He-She made them. Manitou let sunshine into the hole
and this caused the snow on the mountains to melt and rivers and

streams to run. He-She let rain through the hole and the earth drank it, and things grew. He-She made animals. Pieces of his-her cane became fish, for instance. The Ute people used to eat fish but do not any more, because some bad people once threw their dead enemies into the water, and it became impossible to tell the difference between the real fish and the fish that had at one time been people. Manitou went on to make birds out of the leaves of various plants and animals from other parts of his-her cane. All of the animals lived in harmony until Coyote came. But that's another story.

Some Omaha of Nebraska say that in the beginning there was only Wakanda. Everything that would eventually exist lived only as spirits in his mind, which is the space between Heaven and Earth. These spirits wanted very much to take form, and eventually they dropped down to Earth, where they found only water stretching endlessly into the four directions. Everything changed when a fiery rock emerged from the depths, causing water to become clouds and leaving land for the spirits to populate as living beings. The primary effect of this myth is to emphasize the spiritual essence, the sacredness, of the land itself. It is only through earthly elements that spirit can become form.

Earthmaker is the Great Spirit of the Ho-Chunk (Winnebago) people of the upper Midwest. He is similar to Wakanda of the Omaha. According to one myth, Earthmaker became conscious sometime before there was a world. Looking around, he realized he was alone and, feeling lonely, he began to weep. His tears became lakes and rivers. Earthmaker then began to wish for company and elements of life – the earth itself, for instance – came into existence. The creator found some clay and, mixing it with a part of his own body, moulded it into humans, including Mother Earth, the true source of all Native Americans. Again, the emphasis here is on the sacredness of Earth itself.

A confederation of the Siksika, Piegan and Blood tribes of northern Montana and Alberta, Canada, have a creator known as

Napi, or Old Man. According to at least some of these people, Napi created in the *ex nihilo* manner. It seems he had always existed, but suddenly decided to travel the empty world, creating mountains, plants and animals everywhere he went. In the north he made Milk River. After he created the river he lay down to rest, placing stones around his body. The stones are still there. When later, after waking from his rest, he stumbled and landed on his knees, he made two buttes where his knees had marked the earth. These buttes are called 'The Knees' to this day. As he continued north, Old Man made hills and streams and the prairies, as well as prairie

Charles Bird King, 'Portrait of Naw-Kaw, a Winnebago Chief [Holding a Sacred Pipe]', *c.* 1837, colour lithograph from Thomas Loraine McKenney and James Hall, *History of the Indian Tribes of North America* (1838–44).

animals – the bighorn and the antelope. And then he noticed some clay and out of the clay he formed human beings. After creating humans, Napi took the form of a culture hero to teach the people how to live properly and then essentially left them to their own devices, becoming an absent god or simply the Great Spirit as a concept rather than as a personal being. Napi's method of creation, leaving signs on Earth of his having once been there, is similar to the Australian Aborigine tradition of walkabouts by creators in what is known as the Dreamtime.

The Pawnee, originally hunters of the Midwestern Plains, tell a Great Spirit creation myth during the spring renewal ceremony. In that ceremony the sacred medicine bundle is opened and the world is recreated through a dance during which the creation myth is sung. The story begins with Tirawahat (Tirawa), the Great Spirit, as Space. It was Space who organized the gods and the universe. Space created the Sun and the Moon and then set Evening Star in the west as the Mother and Morning Star in the east to chase the star people to the Mother. Then Space made four more stars to serve as the four corners of a new world. Space gave wind, thunder, lightning and clouds to Evening Star, and they made noises of joy and danced as Space worked. The creator dropped a small pebble into the clouds and water appeared, and the four world supporters struck the waters with their clubs, and Earth was formed. Evening Star took Morning Star as a husband and promptly gave birth to Mother of Humanity. Sun and Moon mated and produced Father of Humanity. Evening Star made the first sacred medicine bundle while the clouds, thunder, wind and lightning taught the people – the children of Mother and Father of Humanity – the songs and dances that the Pawnee still perform in ceremonies today. Some people say that Mother is dominant; others say that Morning Star followed Evening Star to her home and, after a great commotion, had his way with her. This etiological myth explains not only the formation of the world but certain elements peculiar to the Pawnee,

Charles Bird King,
*Sharitarish (Wicked
Chief), Pawnee,*
c. 1822, oil on panel.

such as the medicine bundle and the relationship arrangements
between Pawnee men and women.

A type of Great Spirit creation from chaos myth is the *deus faber*
(God as craftsman) creation. In this type the creator is a craftsman,
creating the world using specific techniques such as those of a
potter or a carpenter. In China the creator Pangu uses a chisel and
a hammer to carve out the world. In one Egyptian myth, the creator

34

Ptah makes the world on a potter's wheel. In North America, the *deus faber* myths exist too, particularly in the western regions. There the Mescalero Apache, for instance, tell how the Four Grandfathers set up the world as a tent, using posts to tie down the four corners, representing the four directions. In the important puberty rite, a girl, when she first menstruates, is placed in a sacred lodge built in the form of the created universe, a circle bisected along the four directions. The Cherokee of Oklahoma and the Cahto of California also have *deus faber* creations based on four direction-oriented structures.

An elaborate *deus faber* myth is that of the Yuki Indians of northern California.

The Yuki Great Spirit creator is Taiko-mol (Solitary Walker). In the beginning, say the Yuki, there was only a strange foam on fog-covered waters. Then a song came from the waters and Taiko-mol emerged from them, singing as he created a world. He took a rope and laid it out on the north–south axis. Then he walked along the rope, coiling it as he went, leaving earth behind him. He did this four times, but the water kept coming back to cover the earth until Taiko-mol had the idea of creating four stone columns and planting them in the earth, each one representing one of the four directions. To the posts he attached ropes and stretched them out over the new world. Then he lined the world with whale hide. To see that the arrangement was secure, he shook the structure, causing the first earthquake. Traditional Yuki dwellings were always made according to the original creator's world plan, with the four directional posts, ropes and whale-hide lining. It seems likely that the method of creating dwellings came before the myth, the latter serving to give sacred significance to the former.

The Great Spirit sometimes is represented in Native American creation mythology by avatars who are essentially world parents, usually a Sky Father in association with an Earth Mother, as in the Pawnee myth above. The Earth Mother as a world parent wife of the Sky Father is a common motif in mythology. In ancient Greek myth, Gaia is the wife of Uranos; in Polynesian lore, Papa (Earth) is the wife of Rangi (Sky). Another common motif in the world parent myth is the separation of the paternal sky and the maternal earth. The Krachi people of Togo and Ghana, for instance, say that in the beginning Wulbari (Sky) lay constantly on top of Asase Ya (Earth) and that humans, who lived between them, were forever squirming in discomfort and doing things which irritated Wulbari. So much so that he fled away from his mate. Regarding the ancient Greek source, Hesiod tells how the original Earth goddess, Gaia, was covered every night by her husband, Ouranos (Uranus), the Sky, and their mating produced multiple children. Ouranos' subsequently spiteful actions against his progeny caused so much anger among Gaia and the gods' offspring that the couple's eldest son, Kronos, eventually castrated his father.

Native American world parent myths are less violent. Their purpose is to establish the dominance of Earth even over the Sky Father. The Zuni of western New Mexico say that the Great Spirit's seed impregnated the primordial waters, which gave birth to Sky Father and Earth Mother. Sky Father and Earth Mother embraced and eventually gave birth to all the elements and creatures of the world. Then Earth Mother decided to push Sky Father away, leaving space for the new creation – our world – to flourish.

The Diegueño of what is now San Diego County in California believe that the Great Spirit made the Earth female and the Sky male, and when Sky lowered himself onto Earth the creator and his brother, who lived between them, were nearly smothered. Using tobacco, the creator drove Sky up off Earth and the world had room to develop. Another west coast tribe, the Snohomish, have a myth in which the original people living on Earth complained that they were constantly bumping their head against Earth's mate, Sky. Their solution was to use huge trees to lift Sky away from their Earth mother.

Several elements stand out in the many Great Spirit creation myths of Native America. The Great Spirit himself (or itself) is elusive. Whether or not identified as a being rather than a concept, the Great Spirit is rarely the central factor in creation myths. Native Americans in their myths recognize the Great Spirit as an animistic presence in all aspects of life – the rivers, the trees, the animals,

Unknown artist, She-we-na (Zuni Pueblo) culture, Kachina Doll (Paiyatemu), late 19th century, wood, pigment, horsehair, feathers, wool, hide, cotton, tin and ribbon.

the humans, and good and evil. Unlike the God of Christianity, for instance, the Great Spirit is not the subject of theological issues such as the ultimate nature and meaning of the deity or the deity's relation to the afterlife. In short, there is little or no metaphysical speculation involved. In Great Spirit creation myths the emphasis is on the sacredness of Earth and life rather than on a heavenly god and his power.

The Great Spirit is the animistic power that relates all aspects of creation to each other in harmony. If creation myths attempt to convey animistic power by metaphor, certain rituals provide living, communal expression of that power. The Green Corn ceremony of the Iroquois, Cherokee and several other eastern and southern tribes – a celebration of the year's corn crop – is a rite of renewal,

John White, *The Green Corn Ceremony*, 1585–93, drawing.

atonement and tribal harmony. It is, implicitly, a ceremony that affirms the unifying power of the Great Spirit and the sacredness of all aspects of life. The ritual involves dancing, singing and feasting, and the lighting of a new fire, symbolizing a new beginning, a new creation. The Sun Dance ceremony of the Sioux and other Plains Indians is more dramatic. The ritual often involves acts of sacrifice represented by fasting and even sometimes by painful piercing. Central to the ritual is the smoking of a ceremonial pipe. Again, the purpose of the Sun Dance is renewal and tribal harmony, in effect a re-establishment of the power of the Great Spirit.

One of the most complex renewal rituals is the series of healing 'sings' or 'ways' of the largest Native American tribe, the Dine

George Catlin, *The Cutting Scene, Mandan O-kee-pa Ceremony*, 1832, oil on canvas.

39

Edward S. Curtis, portrait photograph of a Navajo (Dine) medicine man (Haatali) from Canyon de Chelly, c. 1904.

(Navajo). These rituals involve shamans (*hataalii* or medicine men) and their dry (sand) paintings. In the most important of these sings, the Blessingway, the painting, the designs of which are made of coloured sands, is intricately related to the creation myth of the tribe. The painting, and the prayers and songs associated with it, is meant to cure or protect an individual in need, who actually sits in the painting. The Dine word for the Blessingway is *hozhohe*. According to tribal belief, the ritual was given to the people soon after their arrival in the world and was first performed by the gods and especially by the Great Goddess, Changing Woman. The Dine word for 'dry painting' means 'the place where the gods come and go'. In the ceremony of the Blessingway, the painting is intended to attract the gods – the collective essence of the Great Spirit.

The central figure in these rituals of renewal or re-creation is the *haatalii* or medicine man, 'medicine' ultimately being directed not only at the healing of an individual's physical or spiritual illness but at the re-establishment of harmony between the spirit world and the tribe. The shaman is unique because magical powers allow

Edward S. Curtis, photograph of Navajo (Dine) sand painting, Wind Doctor's ceremony, c. 1905.

40

him to move between the earth world and the spirit world. This movement is, by definition, dangerous and out of the ordinary, since the spirit world includes forces for both good and evil. In many tribes the shaman wears a rope tied to a stationary object, a lifeline should he be held unwillingly in the spirit world. A mythological ancestor of the shaman is the mysterious character known to us as the trickster.

TWO

The Trickster

The trickster, a common figure in animistic cultures, is a shapeshifter and a narcissistic rogue. He often takes an animal form. A famous African trickster is Ananse the Spider. In Central Asia, Erlik is a dog. Raven, Coyote, Iktome the Spider and Nanabozho (Michabou, Nanabush) the Great Hare are all Native American examples. The animal forms of tricksters emphasize their feral aspect, their closeness to unbridled nature.

Usually the trickster brings trouble to humans. The first trickster in the Bible is the Devil, who takes the form of a snake and teaches the first humans how to take pleasure from eating the forbidden fruit. The result is the phenomenon of death. Whatever form he takes, the trickster is both creative and dangerous. He is all ego without the tempering influence of the superego. He is the pre-'civilized' aspect of all of us. His appetites – especially for sex – are voracious and unaffected by morality, or conventionality.

The Ho-Chunk (Winnebago) people of the upper Midwest have a cycle of myths about Trickster (Wakdjunga). In one story Trickster was walking along with his long penis coiled up in a box attached to his back. He came to a lake in which the chief's beautiful daughter and her friends were bathing on the other side. 'Ah-ha,' said Trickster, 'there's fun to be had here.' He immediately released his penis and instructed it as if it were a separate being rather than a part of himself. 'Little Brother,' he commanded, 'go into the water and find your way into the princess over there. But go well into her; her friends will try to pull you out.' The penis started to swim across the lake, but Trickster called him back. 'No,' he cried. 'They'll see you.' So he tied a rock around the neck of his penis and sent him off again. This time the rock ensured that Little Brother would sneak unseen along the bottom of the lake,

Unknown artist, ithyphallic Kokopelli, *c.* 1000, petroglyph, southwest of Abó, New Mexico.

Unknown Native artist, 'Ithyphallic Kokopelli Kachina and his Female Companion (*mana*)', illustration from Jesse Walter Fewkes, *Hopi Katcinas, Drawn by Native Artists* (1903).

and soon he successfully entered the princess. Her friends tried to pull the penis out, but they were unsuccessful. When an old woman straddled the penis and punched it with her awl it came out of the girl, rose up and flung the old woman away.

The trickster here is an image of an aspect of human nature. That Trickster's penis is in a box would seem to symbolize restraint in keeping with tribal convention. The fact that Trickster releases it to do his bidding, as if it were a separate being, suggests a more general human failing of self-control. The long penis is an apt metaphor for the lengths people will go to to satisfy their desires. The old woman's punishment to the penis is, in effect, a cautionary message to those who fail to control their inadmissible behaviour.

A long penis is a feature and theme commonly associated with the trickster. A trickster figure of the Hopi and other tribes of the American Southwest is Kokopelli. This hunchbacked flute player, before he became a popular tourist figure, was an ithyphallic one.

Like the Winnebago trickster, he indulged in antisocial sexual activities. In Hopi rituals intended to bring rain and fertility, he is sometimes accompanied by his mate – his *mana*, or female self – who teases men in the crowd, even throwing them onto the ground and pretending to have sex with them. Kokopelli has a strong appetite for young girls. Some say he carries unborn babies in his hunchback or sac; if girls are not careful he will entice them with his 'flute', and then burden them with these unwanted gifts.

One Hopi story has it that Kokopelli lusted after an especially beautiful girl who had already rejected all of the tribe's most handsome men. Undeterred by his ugly appearance as a hunchback, Kokopelli was determined to win the girl. He followed her around the village and noticed that every day at the same time she went to the edge of the mesa to attend to the calls of nature. The trickster knew what to do. He dug a trench from his house to the very spot where the girl squatted every day. Then he used reeds to make a pipe in the trench and when the girl was in position, he sent his very long penis into the pipe and into the girl's vagina. The girl enjoyed the feeling that resulted, and after several days and as many such experiences, she became pregnant and soon delivered a baby boy. The villagers naturally wanted to know who the lucky father was, so it was decided that the men who wished to be the girl's husband must present her with a bouquet of flowers. If the baby reached out for the flowers of a particular man, the chosen male must be the father. The baby, of course, reached for Kokopelli's bouquet. The people were astonished, but the girl readily accepted Kokopelli, and the couple lived together happily, bringing rain and fertility to the tribe. But the men who had vied for the girl remained jealous of the trickster and decided to kill him. Kokopelli got wind of their plans and asked his grandmother for advice. His grandmother was wise and enlisted the help of the goddess Spider Woman.

Spider Woman told Kokopelli that the men would invite him to the kiva, the social and religious gathering place for men, to do some weaving, and then they would kill him. To prevent this, she gave the trickster some powerful medicine, which she commanded he chew and then spray all over the kiva after dark. Kokopelli did as told, and the medicine turned all the men into Kokopelli-like hunchbacks. Thinking they were killing Kokopelli, the men beat up each other, while the trickster hid in the rafters above.

Often the trickster's activities are ultimately self-destructive. For example, the Sioux have a lesson myth featuring Coyote, the most ubiquitous of all Native American tricksters. Coyote was walking along one day with his friend and fellow trickster, Iktome the Spider, when they came upon a rock named Iya, which Coyote recognized as especially connected to the spirit world. Feeling generous and a bit self-righteous, he took off his cloak and draped it over the rock. 'This will keep you warm in the cold weather, my brother,' he said. Later a storm came up, bringing rain and sleet and making the now unprotected Coyote miserable. Huddled in a cave, he begged Iktome to retrieve the cloak from the rock. 'Iya doesn't really need it; he's lived without it for ages.' Iktome went back to the rock and asked for the cloak. The rock refused. 'A gift given is a gift given, and besides, I like the cloak,' he said. Iktome returned to the cave with his message and Coyote was furious. He decided to go back to the rock himself to demand the cloak. 'You'd better be careful,' warned Iktome. 'That rock has special power.' 'Nonsense,' said Coyote, and he went back to the rock. 'Iya, I am freezing; please give my cloak back,' he cried. 'No,' answered the rock. 'A gift given is a gift given.' Even more furious now, Coyote grabbed the cloak. 'That takes care of that,' he shouted. 'Don't be so sure,' answered the rock. Back at the cave, Coyote and Iktome were sunning themselves after the storm when they heard a strange rolling noise. Soon they saw what it was. Iya was rolling towards them, so they ran. The chase was relentless, and when Iktome realized they were about to be caught he took his spider form and disappeared down a mouse hole. But Coyote was not so lucky. The rock rolled over him and flattened him. A rancher came along, saw what he thought was a rug with a coyote depiction and took it home. As tricksters can die and come back to life, Coyote reformed during the night (like the flattened character in so many Looney Tunes cartoons) and in the morning the rancher's wife said she had seen the new rug running away.

Although Iktome the Spider, a popular Sioux trickster, acts more wisely than Coyote in the story above, more often his actions are humorous metaphors for human foolishness. One Lakota Sioux myth explains that in the past, near the time of creation, Iktome was named Wisdom (Ksa) until his destructive nature caused the creator to strip him of that name. And for certain Iktome was clever but not wise, a fact illustrated in this myth of Iktome and the Buffalo.

One day as Iktome was travelling, he came upon an old medicine man who was singing what seemed to be a sacred song. After the singing was finished, a buffalo fell from the cliff above and lay dead before the old shaman. The man explained that it was his song that had brought the buffalo to him for food. Iktome begged the medicine man to teach him the magic song so that he could provide his village with food. Reluctantly, the man agreed and taught the trickster the song. Waiting until he was well out of the medicine man's sight, Iktome sang the song, and a buffalo fell dead at his feet. Leaving the dead animal there, he continued on his way. Twice more he sang the song, and the same thing happened. Again, he left the dead animals in the dirt without bothering to butcher them. The fourth time he tried the song a buffalo fell off a cliff and landed on him. If some coyotes had not come along to eat the meat, Iktome would have been finished.

Iktome almost always pays a price for his cleverness. One time he arranged with a beautiful girl to sleep with him in his tipi. But the trickster's wife realized what was happening. She and the girl traded places so that the trickster slept with his own wife by mistake. When he realized what had happened, the trickster was rewarded with a severe spousal beating.

Angel de Cora (Hinook-Mahiwi-Kalinaka), illustration from *Old Indian Legends* (1901) that features Iktome being showered with red coals after trying to roast a coyote he had found on the prairie thinking it was dead.

Sometimes the trickster was more successful in his sexual exploits. It seems, for instance, that one day Iktome noticed an especially beautiful young woman who radiated innocence. He was determined to sample this fresh fruit, so he dressed himself in the clothes of an elderly woman and sought out the girl. He found her about to cross a somewhat deep stream. Making his voice sound like that of an old woman, Iktome said hello and suggested that they cross the stream together. The girl agreed, and both she and Iktome lifted their dresses and began to enter the water. 'What hairy legs you have,' said the girl. 'It happens with age,' said her companion. As the pair came to deeper water, they lifted their dresses further. 'Your backside is hairy, too,' said the maiden. 'Yes; another sign of old age,' answered the trickster. 'But what's that thing in front?' exclaimed the girl. 'Oh, it's just a growth a bad sorcerer put on me. I wish I could get rid of it,' said our crafty friend. 'Well, I suppose we could cut it off,' suggested the maiden. 'Oh no,' cried the trickster. 'The sorcerer said I could only get rid of it by putting it in the place between your legs.' Iktome, of course, had his way with the poor maiden.

Stories like this, more than anything else, were meant as entertainment, a kind of humorous pornography that might appeal to the imaginations of men restricted by cultural rules. Like other sexual tales of the trickster, it reflects a human – especially a male human – tendency to ignore those rules when desire intrudes.

As strange as it might seem, in many Native American creation myths the original creators leave the details of creation on Earth to tricksters, who thus become culture heroes. Among the Algonquian-speaking peoples of the eastern woodlands of the United States and Canada, for instance, this is especially so. Depending on the tribe, the trickster/culture hero has various names: Nanabozho, Nanabush, Michabou and Glooscap are examples.

In the creation myth of the Ojibwe and related tribes known collectively as the Anishinaabe of the Great Lakes region, the

Unknown artist, Glooscap sculpture in Parrsboro, Nova Scotia.

R. C. Armour, 'Still the Waters Rose', illustration of Nanabozho in the flood, from *North American Indian Fairy Tales* (1905).

original world was created by the Great Spirit, the Gitche Manitou. This was a perfect world, but gradually the people inhabiting it became selfish, and the balance between themselves and their environment was upset. As in so many mythologies around the world, the creator addressed the problem by sending a great flood. Only the trickster, the Great Hare Nanabozho, and a few animals floating on a log survived. One day, the trickster decided to take on the creative role the Great Spirit had abandoned with the flood. He announced that he would dive to the bottom of the flood waters to find some earth to use to start a new world. He remained underwater for a long time but eventually surfaced, though without any dirt. The waters were too deep even for him. The loon, an experienced diver, also tried and failed, as did several other animals, including the mink and the turtle. Finally, the muskrat said he would try. The others laughed at him, but Nanabozho insisted that Muskrat be given the chance to dive. The little animal remained underwater for hours and finally floated to the surface. When Nanabozho pulled him out of the water, dead, he discovered a bit of earth in the diver's paws. Nanabozho placed the earth on the back of Turtle, and, helped with winds sent by the Great Spirit and dancing performed by the other animals, the earth on Turtle's back grew and grew until our world was formed. Muskrat's sacrificial dive and the subsequent growth of earth under the trickster's guidance emphasize the concept of the sacredness of the physical land itself.

The Lenape along the Delaware River, between what is now New Jersey and Pennsylvania, have also preserved an earth-diver creation myth in a late written text, the *Walam Olum* (Red Book). According to their myth, the creator, Kishelamakank, lived alone in the void, but in his mind was a vision of creation, and as he thought specifically of each item of that potential creation, it came into being – lakes, mountains, forests, plants, Grandfather Sun, Grandmother Moon, the spirits, rock, fire, wind and water. The creator left the Great Toad on Earth to keep things in balance, but Toad became corrupted and things fell apart. So the creator sent a flood to start creation over. The good trickster the Great Hare, whose Lenape name was Nanapush, with a few humans in his shirt, managed to survive by climbing a cedar tree on top of a mountain. Nanapush sent animals to dive into the flood waters to find some soil for a new Earth. As in the Anishinaabe myth, the muskrat

Unknown artist, pictograph of Nanabozho (the Great Hare), *c.* 1000, Mazinaw Rock, Bon Echo Provincial Park, Ontario.

succeeded in finding the soil, and Nanapush placed the soil on Turtle's back and used it to begin making a new Mother Earth. In time a tree grew out of the new Earth and humans came from that tree. As for the Great Spirit, he left creation alone, leaving it up to the Great Hare trickster (and now culture hero) to continue the creation process and to teach the new people of Earth (sometimes called Turtle Island).

The Ohlone of northern California also have a creation myth that begins with the end of a previous world in a flood. The myth involves the trickster/culture hero Coyote. During the flood, only one mountain top was left of the old world. On it were three beings: Hummingbird, Eagle and Coyote. After the flood, Eagle took Coyote to meet a beautiful girl in a river and said she was to be the latter's wife. She and Coyote would make new people for the new world. Eagle told Coyote how to make the girl pregnant. Coyote in fact made her pregnant by getting her to swallow one of his lice, but the girl ran away after that and she jumped into the ocean. A second wife came along, and Coyote married her, and together they made a new people. Coyote taught these people the details of living: how to find food, how to procreate and so forth. As in many trickster as culture hero creation myths, the haphazard creation of humans, emphasized here by the loss of Coyote's first wife, is in keeping with a general sense of human imperfection.

The Nez Perce of the Pacific Northwest have a creation myth that also features Coyote, who uses his trickster magic as a monster-slaying hero and creator. When he arrived in the space that would be Earth he confronted a monster there, entering its stomach and lighting a fire within. He killed the monster and allowed the animals it had eaten to escape into a new world, one that Coyote created out of the dismembered pieces of the monster.

Usually Coyote is a less benevolent creator. In a myth of a northwest tribe, the Maidu, he introduced death into creation. The Maidu say that in the beginning Turtle and Earth Initiate created some dry land, the Sun, the Moon, the stars and a large acorn tree. Before long, Coyote and his pet, Rattlesnake, emerged from the earth. Coyote watched with great interest as Earth Initiate made animals and people out of clay. He tried to make some people, copying Earth Initiate, but they were imperfect because he laughed at them as he made them. Meanwhile, Earth Initiate was making a perfect world with baskets always full of food so that no one had to work and no one would ever get sick. When a person became old they had only to jump into a nearby lake to regain their youth.

Then one day Coyote came to visit, and the people told him how easy life was. 'I can show you something even better,' he said. He told them it would be a good thing if people got sick, old and died. The people were confused. Coyote told them it would all be

clear if they had a foot race. Now Coyote's pet, Rattlesnake, hid
in a hole along the proposed race path with just his head sticking
up. The race began and one racer led the way. This happened to
be Coyote's own son. As the boy passed by Rattlesnake, the snake
bit him, and soon he became sick and died. The people thought
he was asleep, but Coyote, who was now weeping the first tears
ever shed in creation, explained that his son was dead. As he dug
a grave, he explained that from now on death would be the end of
each person's life. Coyote's intent here was to introduce death to
the people. But the trickster's plans had a habit of backfiring, which

could lead to unexpected results – in this case, the introduction of sadness represented by tears.

An unusual Coyote creation story is one told by the Crow people of the Great Plains. The tribe's earth-diver creation myth features Old Man Coyote, the creator, and a character known as Little Coyote, who came out of nowhere and worked to undermine and corrupt Old Man Coyote's work. According to the story, Old Man Coyote sent a duck on an earth-diver mission to find some dirt at the bottom of the primordial waters. With difficulty, the duck found some dirt and gave it to Coyote. Coyote breathed on the mud and it grew into a world. Urged on by his duck companions, the creator made plants, valleys, mountains, rivers and the rest of creation – everything except humans. Finally, again urged on by the ducks, he made mankind out of some clay. But Coyote realized he had only made male humans, so he made some females, and everyone had fun multiplying. All went well until one day Coyote came across what appeared to be a miniature version of himself. 'Who are you, Little Brother?' he asked. Little Coyote answered, 'I don't know, Big Brother; I'm just here.' Then Little Coyote began to make suggestions to Old Man Coyote. 'You've only made humans and ducks,' he said. So Coyote made all kinds of other animals and, acting like a true culture hero, taught them how to dance, hunt, cook, dress, make tipis and live together. But Little Coyote was perhaps jealous of the people, and he did a bad thing; he suggested to the creator that he give the people many languages so that they would misunderstand each other. The result was wars between tribes. So the world goes, thanks to Little Coyote.

Among the Moapa and Paviotso of California, Coyote appears in the same role as trickster and creator. In one creation myth of that area there is a woman creator who lives with her daughter in a deserted place. The woman has created the Earth but needs to place people in it. She sends her daughter out to find a husband who can help to make people. The daughter returns with Coyote. Coyote begins to have sex with his new wife but discovers that she has teeth in her vagina. He disarms the vagina, and then after a while the woman gives birth to many babies, which she puts into a small container. She gives the container to Coyote, who distributes them in the world as the first human beings.

An especially complex trickster and creator figure is Raven, probably a product of Central Asia. The Chuckchee people of Siberia, for instance, recognize Raven as a self-creator whose wife produced featherless humans and then challenged Raven to continue the creative process. This Raven did by defecating and urinating the world into existence and then teaching the featherless humans how to copulate. Raven's method of creation is grotesque and suggests an ambiguous and cynical rather than a sentimental or reverent view of creation.

Raven is primarily a figure of the Pacific Northwest. A Raven world-parent creation myth is told by the Alaskan Kodiak Island people. Again, bodily waste plays a role. The Kodiak say Raven

Bill Reid, *The Raven and the First Men*, 1980, laminated yellow cedar.

brought light from the sky, and at the same time a bladder containing the first man and woman came down. The man and the woman created mountains by pushing at the walls of the bladder with their hands and feet. The woman urinated and spat to make rivers and oceans. The man made a knife out of one of the woman's teeth and used it to make woodchips, which he threw into the waters below to make fish. The man and the woman, the world parents, had a son who used a stone as a plaything. The stone turned into the world – that is, Kodiak Island. A second son married a female dog who gave birth to the Kodiak people.

A somewhat milder example of the self-created Raven is found in the creation myth of the Iñupiat of Alaska, where Raven uses his trickster powers primarily as a culture hero. He also, at least indirectly, introduces evil into the world. It is said that at the beginning of time Raven came suddenly into consciousness – that is, became aware of himself in what was then only primeval darkness. He began to explore his own body, becoming aware of what we think of as human characteristics. He also noted the bump on his head which would eventually become his beak when he took on his animal shape. Raven went on to create the elements of life, including his dark side, Tornaq, the first evil spirit, whom Raven threw into the void but who would forever after plague humankind. After his work, including the making of humans, was complete, Raven left his creations to fend for themselves, but only after teaching them how to survive and how to remember him.

In the creation myth of the Tlingit in the Alexander islands of Alaska, Raven uses his trickster capabilities as a culture hero to steal the Sun for his people. Born of the Great Spirit Kit-ka'ositiyi-qa, Raven tried to learn from his father how to create a world. He did learn enough to create a sort-of-world. But his world had no light in it. Raven had heard that there was a being far away who had light hidden somewhere. He decided to use his inborn trickster talents to get that light for his world. He found his way to the house where light was hidden, and he discovered that the owner of the house had a daughter. A natural shapeshifter, Raven turned himself into a grain of sand and dropped into the girl's water glass. Naturally, the girl drank the water and became pregnant. Soon she gave birth to a baby with two very bright, fast-moving eyes. The baby kept crying for the strange bundles that hung on the walls of the house. The people living there became so tired of the crying that they gave the child one of the bundles. He played with the bundle for a while, and soon, when he was bored with it, it floated up out of the ceiling smoke hole into the sky. Once there, it broke open and released a sky-full of stars. Then the baby cried for another bundle, played with it, released it, and watched it float out of the smoke hole. It broke open and the Moon came out. The child cried for another bundle, and the same thing happened. But this time the result was sunlight. Now the baby turned into Raven and flew out of the smoke hole crying 'Ca, Ca'. Raven had successfully stolen the light of the world.

Raven did not stop there. He tricked the owner of a spring into leaving it for a while and then stole its water for his world. And he began to invent all sorts of obscenities and immoral appetites that he then happily satisfied. After that he caused a flood by finding his way into a place where a woman who controlled the tides lived. He made the woman raise the tides so that water covered the earth, destroying all the humans there. These humans became stones after the waters subsided, and Raven made new humans out of leaves. Just as leaves get old and die, these new people grew old and died. These people are the Tlingit.

Given the many sometimes conflicting characteristics of the trickster – his ambiguity – it is no wonder that mythologists and other scholars have long wrestled with his meaning. If a myth is a cultural dream, it makes most sense to assume that a culture dreams the trickster because the trickster is an active aspect of that culture's collective psyche. Consideration of the myths above indicates that the trickster has several psycho-cultural functions. At one level he is a source of entertainment – essentially a walking 'dirty' joke and a reminder of our lack of self-control. When we laugh at the trickster we laugh at aspects of ourselves. At a related level, the trickster is a source of lessons about cultural mores. In the story of the coat and the rock, for instance, Coyote and the listeners of his story learn that there are consequences when a gift given becomes a gift taken away. The trickster's selfishness here and elsewhere reminds us of our own self-centredness. Beyond these points, the trickster's meaning becomes more complex. To the extent that we sympathize with Coyote, Iktome and Raven in their antisocial behaviour, we recognize the necessity of sometimes challenging what can be a stultifying conventionalism in close-knit societies. It is certainly true that as scandalous and chaotic as the trickster is, he is also highly creative. He can overcome most obstacles; he is a transformer even if sometimes he becomes the butt of his own tricks, as in the rock story. To be creative beings, we require something of whatever the trickster's voracious appetites and challenges to the status quo represent. We are taught to keep our unconventional urges under control – represented, for instance, by the Winnebago trickster's penis in the box on his back. But releasing those urges is a celebration of transforming imagination. This brings us to the fact that the trickster in Native American mythology, as in African mythology, often plays a central role in creation myths, usually becoming, in fact, a culture hero who nevertheless retains the ambiguous nature of the trickster, as in the Maidu myth in which Coyote introduces death. This myth and other trickster myths speak to the duality in both human nature and creation.

Duality is evident in other myths in which the trickster and culture hero is divided into two characters. The Anicinape or Omaniwininiwak, a Canadian Algonquian tribe of Quebec, say that it was the Great Earth Mother who played the role of the Great Spirit in creation. The Mother produced two children. After she died, the first child, the good trickster Glooscap, acting as a culture

Hopi Pueblo, Kachina Doll, Koshare Clown, late 20th century, wood, plant fibres, fabric, paint and cord.

Hopi Pueblo, Kachina Doll (Koyemsi [Mudhead]), late 19th century, wood and pigment.

hero, created the elements of life on earth – plants, animals, humans – out of the body of his mother. The second child, Malsum, became the embodiment of the untamed dangerous qualities of the trickster. He introduced death, poisonous plants, aggressive animals and human evil. Again, both aspects of the trickster are parts of what we are and parts of creation as a whole.

Although the trickster is dangerous, he takes a more 'civilized' form in the character of the sacred clown in Native American ceremonial dances. The clowns have many names depending on tribal languages, but whether the Sioux Heyoka, the Zuni Mudeaters, the Cherokee Boogers, the Iroquois False Faces or the Pueblo

Koshare, their functions are universal. Like their trickster ancestors and counterparts, they tend to be lascivious and generally uncontrollable. They say and do things during ceremonies that would be unacceptable outside of those settings. In this way they reverse the normal order of things, revealing the chaotic creative power and the arbitrariness of life itself. Even as they celebrate the appetites, the fertility and opulence of creation, they humiliate tribal members who have failed in some way to follow tribal rules or traditions. As such they are tribal policemen or comic culture heroes, reminding the people of cultural obligations. Like the dancers in the more serious aspects of the ceremonies of which they are at least a peripheral part, they are participants in the cleansing – the ritual re-creation – of the community. Among the clown figures of the Southwest, for instance, is the Hopi clown Kachina or spirit figure known as Mudhead. His close association with the earth is indicated by the mud which decorates his body. It is said by some Hopis that it was Mudhead who led the people out of earth, the mother of us all, into the present world.

In all of the trickster-centred creation myths and clown-based activities in the rituals just mentioned, there is a realistic sense of a world that has imperfection at its source.

THREE

The Goddess

The Earth Mother is a seminal figure in creation mythology. As a world parent she is associated with the creator god or, particularly in matrilineal societies, she stands alone as a dominant power. She is the many 'Venuses' of the ancient Paleolithic world; she is Gaia in Greece, Devi in India, Pachamama in South America, Coatlicue in Meso-America, and she takes many forms in the animistic mythologies of Africa. World-parent creation myths often include the dismemberment of a parent and the use of his or her body parts to make the world. In Norse mythology the original giant, Ymir, is killed by several gods who turn a portion of his body into Earth, his skull into sky, his bones into mountains and his blood into the seas. In Mesopotamia the world parents Tiamat and Apsu are defeated, killed and turned into aspects of the world in a new creation. In some cases, a primordial being is sacrificed as part of a more ritualized act. In Ceram in Indonesia, the maiden Hainuwele is cut up and planted to be eventually harvested as staple plants for her people. In Vedic India the first man, Purusha, is sacrificed to create new life.

The Great Goddess is a major figure in the creation myths of North America. As a world parent she is the Earth Mother, sometimes, literally, Mother Earth. The Okanagan of Washington State say that the Great Spirit made Earth from a woman, the mother of us all. The woman lives still in a new form. Her flesh is the soil,

Nuvualiak Alariak, *Sedna with Fingers Cut*, undated.

her hair the trees and plants, her bones the rocks, her breath the wind. We live on her body. In a Canadian Algonquin myth, Earth Mother dies and her son, the culture hero Glooscap, uses the parts of her body to form the elements of creation. Sometimes in Native American mythology, the death of the Earth Mother is an act of sacrifice which produces essential food without which the created peoples would not survive. An example of this type of myth is the Corn Mother story told by the Penobscot tribe of Maine, a matrilineal people.

In the beginning, according to the story, a being known as First Mother was born of a magical plant fertilized by dew, warmed by the Sun. First Mother mated with a culture hero sent by the Great Spirit and gave birth to the first people. After a while there were too many people and not enough food. First Mother told her husband that the only hope was that she be sacrificed. 'You must kill me and then do what I tell you to do,' she said. The husband at first refused, but the Great Spirit ordered him to do what First Mother demanded. So it was that the husband followed First Mother's precise instructions. He killed her at noon when the Sun was highest in the sky. Then he had her sons drag her body over cleared spaces of earth. The sons were to drag her by her long silky hair, scraping bits of her flesh from her body. Seven moons later, as instructed, the sons came back to the place where they had dragged their mother. To their amazement, they found that the flesh of their mother had returned to life as beautiful tall plants topped by fine silken hair and clustered edible kernels they called corn. First Mother thus became Corn Mother and provided her children with the food they needed to survive.

The message here is clear. Mother Earth's creation is ongoing and cyclical rather than *ex nihilo* and linear. The myth is analogous to agricultural practices in which old plants must be cut down and seeds buried before new plants can be born. The Earth Mother teaches us that to have life on Earth, we must have death. The Earth Mother creates life continually, but she also takes it back to herself.

An incarnation of the sacrificed Earth Mother in the far north is Sedna, a goddess of the Inuit people of northern Canada and Alaska. As the Inuit traditionally survive by hunting and fishing, it is logical that their creation myth says little about an *ex nihilo* creation and emphasizes instead the creation by an Earth Mother of the animals typically hunted. The myth here is a version told by the Oqomiut Inuit people.

It was a male figure named Anguta, who lived with his beautiful daughter Sedna, who is said to have created the world originally. One day Sedna was convinced by a great sea bird, a fulmar, to fly away with him. When she arrived at the bird's home, however, she was disgusted by its filthiness, its foul smell and its lack of food. In desperation, she called for her father, who, after a year had passed, finally arrived, killed the fulmar and took his daughter away in his boat. Soon other fulmars found the corpse of their chief and set off in search of his murderer. When they found Anguta's boat they stirred up a terrible storm. To save himself from capsizing, Anguta threw his daughter overboard, and when she grasped the gunwales of the boat, he cut off her fingers. The fingers fell into the water and became whales and other sea animals. Sedna fell into the sea but survived, and as the storm calmed down she climbed back into the boat. Sedna no longer loved her father, and, when he was asleep, she ordered her dogs to bite off his hands and feet. On waking up, Anguta was furious. He cursed his daughter, the dogs, and everyone and everything in the world. Then the earth swallowed Sedna and her father. Father and daughter live now in a place under the world known as Adlivun; Sedna rules there, and Anguta just hobbles around with no power. When humans die, they go to Sedna's house in Adlivun. People who have lived wicked lives have to sleep with mean old Anguta, who pinches them all night.

In this myth it is the goddess rather than the male creator who possesses the power to continue the creation process. It is Sedna who is the animistic source of the creatures so important to the sea-based hunting practices of the Inuit world. And in keeping with the traditional role of the Earth Mother in other parts of Native America, it is Sedna who, as ruler of Adlivun, takes her people back to her when they die.

Many other Earth Mother creations are found in the earth-diver myths of the eastern half of what is now the United States. In these myths the goddess usually falls from the sky. Versions of the myth are told by the tribes of the Iroquois Confederacy and by others influenced by the Iroquois. Some Mohawk Iroquois, for instance, tell the story in the following way.

There once was a place up in the sky that was a kind of paradise. All the houses there were properly oriented east to west in keeping with the rising and setting of the Sun. There was a woman who lived in one of those houses with a man whose magical powers kept things perfect, the way they were meant to be. But then one day the man died, introducing death to the sky world. Soon the woman was obviously pregnant – also a new state in the sky world – and she gave birth to a girl child named Aientsik (Earth). After a time the child began to cry continually, except when she stood in front of the place where the dead man – her father – was buried. She spent hours talking to her father's spirit, and after some time informed her mother that she was to be married and that her father had instructed her to go to the place of a man called Sky Supporter. So Aientsik's mother packed a basket of fruit and cornbread for her daughter, and the girl set off. Eventually she found Sky Supporter and gave him the basket of fruit and cornbread. But after three days and nights the man became sick. He took Aientsik to a tree – the Tree of Light – and instructed her to pull it up from the ground, as this would cure him of his sickness. This the girl did, and as she looked over into the hole left by the pulled-up tree, Sky Supporter pushed her into it – it was in fact a hole in the sky – and Aientsik began to fall, grabbing corn, bean and squash roots on the way down. As she drifted through the void she saw a huge expanse of water below, with lots of animals floating in it. One of the animals, the loon, looked up and saw the girl, whom the animals called Sky Woman, falling towards them. He told Turtle to let the woman land on its back. The flying animals, the birds, went up to guide Sky Woman's descent. Immediately after landing on Turtle's back, Aientsik told the animals she would need some dirt to start a world. Several of the animals in turn dove into the waters to try to get to some soil. But they failed. Finally, as in the Ojibwe myth discussed earlier, Muskrat dove and succeeded in bringing up a pawful of dirt. Some say he died in the process, but he did drop a small pile of dirt on Turtle's back, and Aientsik walked around the dirt each day until it became land – our world (that is, Turtle Island) – and the roots she had brought with her began to produce edible plants for the people who were born of Aientsik and lived there.

A Cherokee myth follows most of the features of the Iroquoian Sky Woman legend, and says that all the foods came directly from her body after she landed on Turtle. The Cherokee say she also produced the spark of consciousness symbolized by the eternal flame used in tribal ceremonies. An element that makes the Cherokee creation myth significantly different to the Iroquoian version is the presence of the sun as a goddess, known in this tale as Unelanuhi. In world mythology sun goddesses, as opposed to male sun deities, are rare. Other than the Japanese sun goddess Amaterasu, Unelanuhi has few mythological sisters. Some Cherokee see her as a Great Spirit creator, some say the goddess Spider Woman brought her up from the underworld to the sky to give warmth and light to the people. In this sense her significance, like that of other native American goddesses, would seem to be her attachment to earth as opposed to sky. Unelanuhi is a mother who warms the earth.

A Shawnee myth says the Sky Woman was the primary creator. Known as 'Our Grandmother', she descended from the sky, created the turtle for her landing, then created the earth and the sky and everything else. The Shawnee also add a flood myth to the creation story. They say that Our Grandmother's grandson, Cloudy Boy, killed a man by knifing him in the stomach and that from the wound a flood of blood covered the world. When the flood subsided, Our Grandmother created a new world.

In these myths and others like them, the world comes into existence from the Earth Mother rather than from a Sky Father. She leaves the Sky World because she is associated with earthly phenomena such as pregnancy, sickness and death, all elements of the cycles of fertility and life itself foreign to the pre-creation heavenly world. The dominance of the goddess in these myths reflect the matrilineal traditions of the Iroquois, the Cherokee and many other tribes which tell the Sky Woman myth. In these tribes, motherhood is revered: a child takes the mother's rather than the father's name, and, in many cases, belongs to the mother's rather than the father's clan. In what is a dream-like image of a woman floating down from the sky (in a Kiowa myth she uses a rope to descend) and landing on a turtle's back, such elements as the hole from which she emerges, the primordial waters from which the soil is taken, and the midwife-like role of the Earth Mother herself in the creation all suggest a birth metaphor, which are also evident in the emergence creations of the American Southwest.

The emergence myth in its many versions always involves the passage of the first people, by way of a small opening from inside the earth to this world. The symbolism here is evident. The people are 'born' of the earth, the universal mother. Although many cultures in the world recognize the importance of Mother Earth, the emergence myth as such is most fully developed in the Americas, especially in the southwest region of North America among the Pueblo peoples, many of whom are matrilineal, and the Navajo, who are also matrilineal. For the Pueblos the birth metaphor is architecturally and ceremonially always present. Central to Pueblo religious life is the kiva building – often underground – in which

sacred ceremonies and other social activities take place. In the floor is a small opening, the *sipapu*, to mark symbolically the place of emergence. And in ceremonial dances, the participants begin by emerging from the hole at the top of the kiva, reminding everyone present of the original birth from the Earth Mother.

Associated with most of the emergence creation myths is a goddess figure who differs among the tribes and has many names. Among the Keres and Tewa Pueblo peoples of New Mexico, she is Prophesying Woman, Thinking Woman (Tsichtinako) or Old Spider Woman. Further west among the Hopi she is Spider Woman, Spider Grandmother, or Hard Beings Woman (Huruing Wuhti). For the Dine (Navajo) she is Changing Woman, and for their Athabascan relatives to the south, the Tinde (Apache), she is White Painted Woman or White Shell Woman.

Pre-Pueblo builders, a kiva with a fire pit hole and a *sipapu* (the smaller hole in the floor), *c.* 1000, Long House Ruins in Mesa Verde National Park, Colorado.

upper world. 'What was it like?' the girls asked. 'Flat,' answered Locust. As punishment for his disobeying them the sisters said he would have to live in the ground and would have to die and be reborn every year.

Now Tsichtinako said it was time for the sisters to emerge. So the girls took the baskets and Badger and Locust, climbed the pine tree to the hole above, and broke through into the upper world. There, as instructed by Tsichtinako, they waited for the Sun to rise in what the goddess had told them was the east. Then, for the first time, they sang the song of creation, which the people still sing today. Tsichtinako told them about the other three of the four directions and also told them that their father was Uchtsiti, who had created the world from a clot of his blood. She explained that creation was to be completed by them. They were to plant the seeds in their baskets and to give life to the animal models there. This the girls did, but they were afraid when darkness came, until Tsichtinako explained to them about night and day. When the sisters had completed the creation, they took the names Iatiku (Life-bringer) and Nautsiti (Full Basket).

Acoma is a matrilineal culture in which ownership is passed down through the female line. It is not surprising, therefore, that the Acoma creation myth is dominated by female figures. At the centre of the myth is the concept of female power in the universe. Given this concept, it is logical that the beginning of the process by which the world as we know it was created occurs inside the symbolic womb of the Great Mother, personified by the goddess Tsichtinako. Although we are told that the original creation came from the blood of a male creator, we hear nothing more about that creator. The concern of the Acoma myth is with the earth itself and the birth of our world from that earth rather than from a dominant sky god or Great Spirit. The father god provides the seed of creation, but it is the earth goddess who gives birth to and nurtures the people. The importance of the earth and the universal female force it represents is reflected in Pueblo dances such as the corn and harvest dances in which the feet of the men pound insistently on the earth, calling on it to be productive while the feet of the women dancers shuffle familiarly close to their sister, confident of her gifts.

A goddess well known to all the southwestern tribes, and particularly important to the Hopi, the Zuni and the Navajo, is Spider Woman, or Spider Grandmother. She is also recognized in other parts of the country. The Coos of Oregon, the Ojibwe of the

Unknown Hopi artist, 'Palahiko Mana Kachina (Water Drinking Maiden)', a form of the Corn Maiden figure, illustration from Jesse Walter Fewkes, *Hopi Katcinas, Drawn by Native Artists* (1903).

northern United States and southern Canada, and the Choctaw of the Southeast all have Spider Woman myths. It was Spider Woman, for instance, who gave fire to the Cherokee.

Spider Woman is the central figure in the Hopi emergence. Hopi myths, like those of all Native Americans, were originally passed on orally, and in the Hopi Reservation there are several villages with their own distinct mythological and religious traditions. The story that follows here, then, is one of many versions a visitor to Hopi might hear.

In the beginning there was only empty space and Tawa the sun spirit. Tawa began to create what would be a First World under the ground. This world was inhabited by insect-like creatures who lived in caves and spent most of the time fighting with each other. So Tawa sent a another spirit, Spider Grandmother – really a part of himself – down to the First World to help the people make what would be a long journey to a Second World. During the trip the people took on new forms as animals, such as wolves, dogs and bears. But in the Second World the people still failed to live properly, so Tawa sent Spider Grandmother to lead them to a Third World, where the people now became like real people. Spider Grandmother urged them to live there in harmony. She taught them to build villages, to grow corn, to weave and to make pots. But the world was cold, and nothing worked very well. Discord was everywhere. There was no harmony. Once again Spider Grandmother arrived and suggested to the people who still had good hearts that they should move to a Fourth World, a world up on the surface of Earth. The chief of these people and some other elders prayed and practised various ceremonies and then made a swallow and asked it to find a way to the upper world. The swallow flew up and did find an opening, but winds forced it back down. So the chief and the wise men made a dove and sent it to explore. The dove made it to the upper world and came back to report to the chief that the upper world had no life. The chief sent a hawk up and the hawk came back with the same impression. Now the chief sent a catbird. The catbird met Masauwu, a katsina or spirit, the strange keeper of fire and the master of the Fourth World. He said the people could come to his world, but the people had no way of climbing up to the hole at the top of the Third World. Again, Spider Grandmother came to the rescue. She suggested that Chipmunk, who regularly ate pine nuts, might be able to help them plant a pine tree that would reach the hole. The chipmunk agreed to help and planted some pine nuts. Soon a spruce tree grew, but it was too short to be of any help. A fir tree grew, too, but it was again not tall enough. The same problem existed with a white pine. Finally, the people tried a hollow bamboo reed. Spider Grandmother told the people to sing a certain song to make the reed grow taller, and in time it matured enough to reach the opening, the *sipapu*. The chipmunk told the people to climb up through the hollow reed. So, led by Spider Grandmother, the people entered the Fourth World, the world where the Hopi live now.

As in the Acoma myth, the creative force here is the feminine power represented by Spider Grandmother. Tawa, the original creator, is a personification of the Sun, but he is a figure withdrawn from the people. The primary concern of the myth is with the Earth, the world of Spider Grandmother, the Hopi version of the Earth Mother.

The primary goddess and Earth Mother of the largest North American tribe, the Navajo (Dine), is Changing Woman (Estsanatlehi). An Athabascan people whose ancestors lived in western Canada and Alaska, the Navajo began to arrive in small groups in what is now New Mexico and Arizona in the 1300s. By 1400 they had established relations with the Pueblo people, whose mythology they absorbed and reworked into what is, in effect, a complex oral epic of emergence and migration. The mythology and related ceremonies discussed earlier serve the Navajo and their Athabascan relatives, the Apache, as metaphors and vehicles for an ever-present creation process by which the unwell or corrupted individual or

Overleaf: Spider Rock (the home of Spider Woman), Canyon de Chelly National Monument, Arizona.

77

tribe moves from disintegration to moral integration and spiritual wholeness (*hozho*). At the centre of these myths and rituals is Changing Woman, whose name reflects her ability to move, like the seasons of Earth, from old age to youth and back again. Changing Woman cures, and curing for the Navajo is a re-creation, a second chance, a movement from death to rebirth. For any Navajo curing ceremony to be effective, it must contain a chant from the larger story of the Blessingway, the collection of chants that feature Changing Woman and creation.

It is said by the Navajo that in what was a monster-dominated period after the emergence, First Man and First Woman found a tiny, perfectly formed turquoise girl during a storm on Giant Spruce Mountain (Gobernador Knob), and they raised the child. When the girl achieved her first menses, First Man and First Woman organized a four-day ceremony to celebrate. To begin, First Woman took the role of a figure known as Ideal Woman and adorned the girl with fine jewels – beads of turquoise, coral and other stones. Then she dressed her in a fine white woven dress and moccasins and leggings. This young woman was, in fact, Changing Woman.

Edmond L. Tracey (Navajo), *Cloud Gods*, 20th century, watercolour on paper.

Each day of the four-day ceremony the young woman ran towards the Sun in the east, and each day Ideal Woman massaged her from head to toe, bringing her into the strength of womanhood, preparing her later to conceive by the Sun the hero twins, who would make the world safe for the people.

The Changing Woman story provides the events for the Navajo Kinaalda ceremony, the four-day celebration recognizing the coming of Navajo girls into womanhood. A similar ceremony, the Sunrise Ceremony, welcomes Apache girls at puberty. In the Kinaalda, the Navajo girl becomes Changing Woman (the Apache girl becomes White Painted Woman), taking on the goddess's fertility and curative powers. The four days represent the four directions and the four seasons. During the four days the girl will act out the events of the Changing Woman myth. She will wear the ritual clothes and jewels, run each morning to the Sun, and be massaged each day into womanhood. Part of the ceremony involves the girl baking a corn cake symbolizing the fact that, as the cake comes from corn and corn from Mother Earth, the girl, like Changing Woman, now has the goddess's changing powers, turning elements of earth into food.

Goddesses like Tsichtinako and Spider Woman, Changing Woman and Corn Mother are possessed of what Native Americans call 'medicine'. The Native American concept of medicine involves medicine men and women, and objects such as medicine bundles, medicine wheels, sweat lodges, sand paintings as well as the use of special herbs. Medicine as practised by the Native North American tribes involves much more than the curing of individual illnesses. Native American medicine is a spiritual reality, a mystical energy present in certain sacred objects, people or ceremonial activities. Medicine men and women do apply their skills and shamanic powers to individuals, but the goal of all the variant tribal medicines is the physical, spiritual and psychological health of whole communities. As discussed earlier, the Navajo shaman, for instance, sings

Ansel Adams,
photograph
of a Navajo girl
in Canyon
de Chelly,
c. 1941.

sacred ceremonial songs, which are intended to cure psychological or spiritual illnesses and even to ensure the success of various rites of passage such as birth or puberty, but the concept behind these ceremonies is the larger, more general tribal goal of *hozho*, or spiritual and mental harmony.

The Pueblos of the Rio Grande celebrate and maintain their tribal identity in a cycle of ceremonial dances. The Sun Dance of several Plains Indian tribes is a complex event celebrating rebirth and renewal for the society. The Algonquian *Midewiwin* (Great Medicine) is a rite in which individuals are symbolically killed so they and, by extension, the whole tribe can die of sickness and return to wholeness.

The basis of tribal medicine is revealed in myths. At the centre of the Navajo Blessingway rites are the tribe's creation myth and the goddess Changing Woman. The Sacred Arrows rite of the Cheyenne, an Algonquian tribe of the Great Plains, is explained by the myth of the hero named 'Sweet Medicine', who gains sacred knowledge inside a mountain, where he obtains the arrows for what will be the rite. For some Plains Indians the medicine rite is known as the Sun Dance, in which an actual or symbolic self-sacrifice and renewal are central. The rite is related to the myth of the hero, Star Boy (for some tribes he is Scarface, Lodge Boy or other Boys). Star Boy dies

Unknown artist, '[Ojibwe] Herbalist Preparing Medicine and Treating Patient', illustration from J. W. Powell, *Seventh Annual Report of the Bureau of Ethnology to the Secretary of the Smithsonian Institution, 1885–86* (1891).

when a snake enters his body, but he is magically resurrected when the Moon Father sends rain to revive him.

An object commonly associated with Native Americans and their medicine is the so-called peace pipe, more accurately described as a medicine pipe. There are many types of medicine pipes, but a particularly important one is the Calf Pipe of the Lakota Sioux. The smoking of the Sioux pipe represents the relationship between all aspects of creation, with the creator, the Great Spirit Wakan Tanka, being the Great Medicine itself. The inhaling of the tobacco smoke from the pipe is a blessing on the community and on life.

The myth of the Calf Pipe's origins is the myth of Buffalo Calf Woman, the de facto culture hero and goddess of the Sioux, who taught the people what the pipe symbolized, how to use it and how to live properly. The story of Buffalo Calf Woman has been told by many religious leaders, including the famous Sioux holy man Black Elk. This is one of many versions of the myth.

It was a cold day a long time ago. Two Lakota hunters were out looking for game to feed their hungry people. One hunter was good-hearted; the other was not. The men had just about given up on their hunt when something strange happened. A mysterious figure seemed to be coming towards them from the distance. As the figure came closer the men saw that it was a beautiful woman carrying a medicine bundle. The bad-hearted hunter told his companion that he wanted the woman. The good-hearted man said that this desire was shameful as the woman was clearly from the holy *wakan* (medicine) world. As the woman came near to the hunters she beckoned to the bad-hearted one, who approached her with lust in his heart and mind. The hunter and the woman were suddenly covered in mist from which came the sound of hissing snakes. When the mist cleared the bad-hearted hunter, reduced to a pile of bones, lay at the woman's feet.

Now the holy woman instructed the good hunter to return to his chief to tell him of her arrival. She said the people should build

a large ceremonial circle (some say a giant tipi) for a tribal meeting. When the place was ready, the chief told the people to put on their best buckskin garments and to gather there. The people did this, and soon the mysterious woman approached from the far distance. When she finally got there, she circumambulated the ceremonial circle and then stood before the chief. She held the medicine bundle before her and announced that it contained a sacred pipe. She removed the pipe from the bundle and held it up before the people. The bowl was Earth herself, she said, the Great Mother. The tobacco pinches placed in it were the elements of creation. The stem was all the things that grow on the Earth. The beautiful feathers hanging on the pipe were from the Spotted Eagle, representing the flying creatures. The woman taught the people the seven pipe ceremonies: the Vision Quest, the Sweat Ceremony, the Sun Dance, the Ghost Keeping Ceremony, the Ball-throwing Ceremony, the Relative-making Ceremony, and the Isnati Awicalowanpi (the female puberty ceremony). She reminded them that by smoking the pipe they became one with all things in creation. It was through the pipe smoking that their voices – their prayers – would reach the Wakan Tanka. The pipe, she said, must be treated with the greatest respect. To give up reverence for the pipe would be to lose the tribe's identity as a nation.

Plains peoples culture, ceremonial peace pipe without a bowl, possibly 18th century.

The holy woman once again circumambulated the meeting circle and vowed that one day she would return. Then the people were astonished to see that, after resting on the ground for a moment, she arose as a black buffalo, transformed next into a brown buffalo and then a red one before finally becoming a beautiful white calf. To this day the people wait for the return of White Buffalo Calf Woman and regularly perform the sacred pipe ceremony. Whenever a white buffalo calf is born, the people take the birth as a sign that their prayers have reached the Wakan Tanka.

Oscar Howe, *White Buffalo Calf Woman*, 1941, mural, Mobridge City Auditorium, South Dakota.

FOUR

The Hero

Heroes are the embodiments of cultural values, the protagonists of the cultural dreams we call myths. If gods typically remain distant from humans, heroes share our experience of life. They may be better and stronger than we are, but they can only be considered heroes if they take on our form and our experience. Heroes exist at the edge of human possibility. Whether culture heroes, traditional, mythical heroes or historical heroes, they challenge us to transcend our personal and cultural limitations.

Culture heroes are representatives of deities; they instruct newly created communities on how to live, hunt, reproduce, perform certain ceremonies and talk. The Chinese Yellow Emperor taught his people how to write, how to use the bow and arrow and how to govern. Moses led his people to the Promised Land and transferred sacred law to them. Kaang, the culture hero of the San (Bushmen) of South Africa, created game for his people to hunt and taught them proper hunting techniques.

More traditional heroes who are born of women and whose unusual lives make the re-creation of communities possible are represented in mythology by figures such as the Mesopotamian Gilgamesh, the Greeks Odysseus and Theseus, the Meso-american Quetzalcoatl and the Celtic King Arthur. Heroes such as these are recognized by certain signs. They are often conceived miraculously,

Unknown Tlingit artist, ceremonial face mask, 19th century, alder wood.

perhaps to indicate that they belong to the whole culture rather than to any single family. Jesus is born of a virgin; the Buddha is conceived in his mother's dream; Quetzalcoatl is conceived when the great god breathes on his mother; the Irish hero Cúchulainn is conceived when his mother swallows a fly that is really the sun god. Extraordinary childhood deeds can also mark the hero: at six years old Cúchulainn kills a giant hound; in his youth, Arthur pulls the sword from the rock. The child hero is often challenged by a king, who represents the status quo, and is thus a threat to a society's renewal. Religious figures such as the Buddha, Jesus and Zoroaster experience such struggles. The hero's adult life usually involves a quest: Gilgamesh seeks eternal life; Odysseus seeks home and wife; Theseus leaves home in search of a father. The quest is a maze of obstacles, often involving the saving of a community by the killing of a monster. St George kills the dragon; Beowulf kills Grendel. Sometimes an element of the quest is a descent to the underworld, a direct experience of death. This is the case in the stories of Odysseus, Jesus, Gilgamesh and the Roman hero Aeneas. In one way or another, these heroes manage to overcome death to achieve some form of re-creation, a new possibility for the given culture.

In addition to culture heroes and more traditional mythological heroes, there are, of course, historical heroes, men and women who stand as symbols of change and the capabilities of the human spirit. George Washington is an American hero; Joan of Arc is a French hero; Atatürk is a Turkish hero. Of course, one culture's hero can be another's arch-villain.

Culture heroes are frequently present in Native North American creation and re-creation myths. In a Blackfoot myth mentioned earlier, the creator himself, Napi, takes on the role. For the Sioux and other related tribes of the Great Plains, White Buffalo Calf Woman is clearly, in effect, a culture hero sent by the Great Spirit to bring new life to a people. As also noted earlier, many Native American culture heroes are ambiguous in that they are also tricksters. Nanabush (also known as Nanabozho, Glooscap or the Great Hare) is a trickster and culture hero of many Algonquian tribes. Coyote is an even more ambiguous culture hero for tribes such as the Maidu and Crow. And Raven personifies three roles – culture hero, creator and trickster – for many northwestern tribes. Culture heroes often perform deeds that we associate with more traditional heroes. The ones who are also tricksters use their transformative powers to steal such necessities as light and water, as Raven does in the northwestern myths, or they slay creation-threatening monsters, as Coyote does in the Nez Perce myth.

The story of the Great Hare as a monster slayer is a good example of the culture hero/creator. For the Passamaquoddy, Micmac and Maliseet of the northeastern woodlands and southern Canada, the Hare has many names but is perhaps best known as Glooscap. This is one version of his story.

Glooscap had amazing powers. He had created animals and people, a wonderful village, a fine spring with perfect water, and lots of animals to hunt and fish to catch. He had taught everyone how to live together in the right way. With his powers, he could even turn a man into a tree if he wanted to. After all this, he finally decided that it was time to go off into the clouds.

But one day the spring he had left dried up. The people were desperate. They held a council meeting and sent a man northwards to search for the source of the spring, hoping he would find out what was causing the drought. It took the man a long time; he had to walk for many miles until he came to another village. There, what had been a mere spring in his village became a wide stream. But the water in the stream was yellow and foul-smelling. Still, the man was thirsty, and he asked for some of the water. The people refused, saying he would have to go further upstream to ask their chief, who was the owner of the stream. After another long walk, the man came to the home of the chief and was horrified at what he saw. The chief was, in fact, a monster, so huge that his face was far from the ground, up in the sky. And the monster had dammed up the stream and somehow made it foul. 'What do you want?' the monster snarled. The man asked for some water and explained how the spring in his village had dried up because of the monster's dam. 'And we want our water to be clean,' he said. The monster glared at the man and he roared that he did not care about the man or his village. As the monster ranted the man could see inside his mouth all of the things that he had eaten. The man ran off before the monster could eat him, too. Back in his village the man reported to the council that there was nothing they could do.

Of course, Glooscap, even though he was far away, heard all of this and decided he had to do something about it. He painted

Tomah Joseph, 'Glooscap Turning a Man into a Cedar-tree', illustration in Charles G. Leland, *The Algonquin Legends of New England* (1884).

his body, put many feathers in his hair, and stamped his feet so hard that the whole Earth trembled. His fierce war cry was so loud that the mountains shook. He took one of those mountains in his hand and made it into a giant knife. And then he headed for the lair of the monster. Once there he announced that he planned to take clean water to his people. The monster cried out that the water was his and that he would kill Glooscap rather than give it up. The fight that resulted split open the earth and splintered the forests. The monster opened his huge mouth to swallow his attacker, but Glooscap used his knife to slice open the fiend's stomach, and out poured a wide river with plenty of fine water for the villages. He flung the monster into a swamp, where it became a bullfrog.

Another kind of monster slayer is the Blackfoot Indian hero Kutoyis (Bloodclot Boy). Kutoyis embodies the basic components of the traditional mythic hero. He is miraculously conceived and born, he matures quickly, proves his power, undertakes a major quest and defeats a monster. His deeds make possible the survival or re-creation of his people, a process symbolized by his resurrection. This is his story.

There was once a couple who lived happily with their two daughters down where the two creeks come together. The family did lots of hunting and fishing and had plenty to eat. But the man realized he was getting old and would not be able to provide for his family forever. So he was happy when a young hunter came one day to his camp. The old man immediately gave the young man his two daughters as wives and then gave him all of his possessions, except for a tiny lodge in which he and his wife would live. In return, the young man promised to give the old couple all of the meat they would need and enough hides for their clothing and bedding. For a while this arrangement worked just fine. The young hunter became so successful that he captured a whole herd of buffalo that he kept under a logjam down on the creeks. Whenever meat or hides were required, the young hunter would have his old father-in-law jump on the logjam, frightening a buffalo and causing it to run out where the hunter could shoot it.

But the young man began to be stingy with his buffalos. He stopped giving the old man and woman their share of meat and hides, even though he still made the old man help him by stamping on the logjam. And he warned his two wives not to complain about what he was doing to their parents. This was fine with the older daughter, who was mean anyway, but it was not fine with the younger daughter, who regularly stole a bit of meat and took it to the old people.

One day, the young hunter summoned the old man to stamp on the logjam. When he stamped, a buffalo ran out and the hunter shot it. But the shot did not kill the animal, and it ran away bleeding. The old man followed the wounded buffalo and came to a place where there was a large clot of the animal's blood. He quickly put the clot in his arrow quiver and hurried home. 'Quick,' he said. 'Put the kettle on; I have something to cook and eat.' When the water was boiling, he tipped his quiver over and the clot of blood fell into the pot. But immediately there came the sound of a child crying. The old couple peered into the pot, and there in the water was a baby boy. They pulled the child out and made a cradleboard for him. They talked about a name for the boy but quickly realized that if the young hunter thought they had produced a son, he would kill him, because the boy would surely grow up to be a rival. The old couple decided to tell the hunter and his wives that the new child was a girl. They named the child Kutoyis (Clot of Blood).

When the hunter and his wives came home to the camp that day, they heard a baby crying. The hunter sent his wives over to the little lodge to see what was going on. The wives each came back saying that their parents had had a baby girl. Thinking the baby could grow up and become another wife, the hunter instructed his wives to take some pemmican to their mother every day to ensure that she would produce plenty of milk for the baby.

On the fourth day of its life, the child spoke, instructing the old woman to tie him in turn to each of the lodge's four support poles. 'When I am on the fourth pole I will be grown up,' he announced. The woman did as she was told. At each pole, each representing one of the four directions, the boy grew, and when the woman finished tying him to the fourth pole Kutoyis released himself and was now a grown man. He looked around and said, 'There isn't much food in here, but I think there is plenty across the camp at the other lodge.' The old couple explained how the hunter had taken away their arrows and how he did not share food with them. Kutoyis was furious. He and the old man made new arrows and then went to the logjam and killed a buffalo. Hearing the commotion, the hunter came out of his lodge and saw the old man butchering the buffalo. He did not realize that the now fully grown 'baby girl' was hiding behind the buffalo carcass. From there Kutoyis told the old man what to say if the hunter made threats. This the hunter did: 'Breathe deeply, old man,' he said, 'because it will be your last breath.' Coached by Kutoyis, the old man answered, 'Maybe the last breath will be yours.' At this, Kutoyis stood up and used the newly made arrows to kill the hunter. Then he killed the hunter's wives and took all of their food supplies to the old woman.

'Now I have to go on a journey,' Kutoyis said. 'Where can I find people?' The old man told him that there were lots of people over at Badger Creek. So Kutoyis went there. In the middle of the camp was a fine lodge with a painting of a bear on it, clearly the chief's lodge. But Kutoyis went to a much simpler lodge belonging to two old women, who told him how the chief, the Great Bear, mistreated the people. Immediately, Kutoyis went to the chief's buffalo hold and killed and skinned one of the animals. He told the women to take the meat and skin to their lodge. When the chief heard of this he came to the women's lodge with his fellow bears and were about to take the meat for themselves when Kutoyis emerged and killed them all – all except a young female bear whom he sent into the woods to give birth to new bears.

Kutoyis found more people at a camp on the Sun River and discovered a hut belonging to an old woman. The woman told him about the Great Snake Chief and his followers, who were oppressing the people. Kutoyis confronted the chief and his people and killed them all, except one young female whom he sent out into the woods to breed normal snakes.

The villagers told Kutoyis about a terrible monster called Wind Sucker, who was terrorizing the people who lived in the mountains. Kutoyis went there and found the monster. Inside of the monster's wide open mouth Kutoyis could see many people, some dead, some still alive, some only bones. He leapt into the monster's mouth, and asked, 'What's that thing hanging from the ceiling?' 'It's his heart,' the people answered. 'Well, then, we'll do a Ghost Dance,' he said. First he attached a knife to his headdress. Then they all danced around Kutoyis, who danced wildly, the knife piercing the monster's heart with each leap. The monster died, and Kutoyis freed the people who were still alive.

Kutoyis wanted to meet all the people. He found some who lived not far away, but the passage to them was guarded by an evil woman who insisted on wrestling with anyone who tried to get by her. She always won and she always killed her victims. But Kutoyis by now realized that his role in life was to rid the world of evil so that a new harmony, a new creation, could be established. He figured out how to win the wrestling match with the woman, and he killed her. When he proceeded on to the next village he found an evil witch whom he also killed, and finally he came to a village where the worst monster of all lived. This was the Man Eater. Kutoyis dealt with the Man Eater in a strange manner. He met a little girl outside of the Man Eater's lodge and told her he intended to enter the lodge to be eaten. He instructed the girl to retrieve his bones after the monster's meal was done and to throw them to the dogs. She was then to cry out, 'Kutoyis, the dogs have your bones.'

Kutoyis went into the lodge where Man Eater, a fat young man, was sitting, and the monster immediately cut his throat, cooked Kutoyis's body in a pot and ate him. When the little girl asked for the hero's bones, Man Eater agreed. When she threw the bones to the dogs and said, 'Kutoyis, the dogs have your bones,' something amazing happened. Kutoyis rose up from the bones and returned to Man Eater to be eaten again. This happened four times, after which Kutoyis entered the lodge and killed the monster who had threatened the survival of all the people. The fact that the hero chooses to be eaten four times rather than once – each time to the little girl's cry of 'the dogs have your bones' – suggests a medicine ritual associated with the myth, a ritual such as the Ghost Dance in which Kutoyis participates inside of Windsucker. Such rituals were associated with the larger Ghost Dance movement developed

Amédée Forestier, 'The Ghost Dance of the Sioux Indians in North America', from *Illustrated London News*, 3 January 1891.

by Plains tribes in the nineteenth century. The purpose of the somewhat mystical movement, which emerged from the visions of holy men and certain chiefs, was intended to help renew the Earth and to recreate the unity and strength of the tribes in the face of decimation by disease and conquest. The Ghost Dance ritual itself is a dance in which participants move in a circle around a centrally placed pole, sometimes with accompanying drums. The dancers can use the ritual to enter into a trance, but the essential purpose is to envision a future in which the tribes return to the state that existed before the arrival of the European invaders. The U.S. government became increasingly disturbed by the Ghost Dance movement as a threat to its authority over the Sioux in particular. Fearing a rebellion, and suspecting the famous Chief Sitting Bull of being a central figure in the movement, soldiers tried to arrest him on 15 December 1890 and killed him in the process. In so doing, they created an Indian hero-martyr.

The miraculous conception and birth of Kutoyis, his confrontation with monstrous beings antagonistic to life and creation, his experience of death and his miraculous resurrection are reminiscent of the lives of other heroes. Theseus, Quetzalcoatl and Jesus are examples. It is the hero who saves a corrupt world and makes a new creation possible. And Kutoyis is not alone among mythic Native American heroes whose lives are metaphors for such re-creation.

In the complex Navajo creation myth, figures who stand out as heroes are the twin sons of the great goddess Changing Woman. Twins are important figures in many mythologies, including those of the Aztec and Mayan in Meso-America. In Greece and Rome they were the Dioscuri, Castor and Pollux. The story of the Navajo twins is in the Monsterway section of the Blessingway. It contains many familiar elements of the universal mythic hero life, including the miraculous conception and birth and the slaying of creation-threatening monsters, not to mention another important element of many heroic quests: the search for the father.

David Francis Barry, portrait photograph of Chief Sitting Bull holding a peace pipe, 1885.

98

The Navajo myths say there was a time when monsters had pretty much taken over the world. There were the Bird Monsters, the Monster that Kicked People off the Cliff, the Monster that Killed With his Eyes, the Horned Monsters and many others. The people were unable to survive. Only First Man, First Woman and a few others remained. One day, as noted in Chapter Three, the couple found a small piece of turquoise shaped like a female. This figure would become Changing Woman (Estsanatlehi). One day the young Changing Woman, quickly grown up, felt lonely. She lay down on a flat rock near a waterfall. Her feet faced east and the sunshine filled her with warmth. In a short time she gave birth to twins. The twins, Monster Slayer (Nayenezgani) and Born for Water (Tobadzhistshini) as they came to be known later, grew in strength quickly and could even outrun the fastest of the gods. They wondered who their father was, but Changing Woman would not tell them, saying simply that their father was dangerous. Meanwhile, the monsters were everywhere. One approached Changing Woman's dwelling and demanded that she give him her sons to eat. She said she had no sons, and the monster left. But soon many monsters surrounded the house and only a great storm sent by the gods chased them away.

The twins were curious about the world and enjoyed exploring. One day they came to a hole in the ground out of which a column of smoke arose. The boys peered down the hole and saw Spider Woman. She invited them in and asked who they were. They could say who their mother was, but they did not know the name of their father. Spider Woman told them their father was the Sun and explained that the way to his house was treacherous. They would have to walk through rocks that crushed travellers and hot sands that would burn them. But Spider Woman said she would help them get to their father by giving them certain charms that would protect them on their way. She also warned them that the Sun would not be happy to see them, and she taught them how to pass the trials that their father would certainly place in their way. Because of

Spider Woman's help and directions, the twins managed to get to the house. There they met the Sun's wife and announced that they were her husband's children. The wife did not like hearing this, and she hid the boys. When the Sun, tired from a day's work, came home, his wife revealed the twins and asked him directly, 'Whose sons are these?' The twins explained how they had come on what was a dangerous journey to meet their father. The Sun responded that he could not recognize them as his sons unless they could accomplish certain difficult deeds. These included smoking killer-strength tobacco, eating poisoned cornmeal, enduring a white-hot sweat bath, and surviving being thrown against a wall of sharp flints. Thanks to Spider Woman's magic, the twins made it through these ordeals, and the Sun accepted them as his sons. He offered the boys many gifts – jewels, wild animals, domesticated animals, corn and squash plants. But the twins said they would accept those things later. Right now they needed weapons so they could destroy the monsters that were tormenting the world. The Sun eventually agreed and gave them two kinds of lightning and suits of flint armour. He then sent them back to the world on a bolt of lightning.

The twins first confronted Big Giant, who lived near Mount Taylor. With the protection of Spider Woman's magic and their father's lightning, the boys killed the giant and cut off his head. The monster's blood gushed out into the valley, forming a black mass that we can still observe today: what white men call lava. After that, the twin who would take the name Monster Slayer killed many of the other monsters.

Now the twins came to a place below ground where some other monstrous creatures lived. These were named Hunger, Poverty, Sleep, Lice Man and Old Age. The twins were about to kill them but spared them after each one explained why he should be allowed to live. Hunger said he would be necessary to keep people eating. Poverty pointed out that it was he who could make people look for new and better ways to clothe themselves. Sleep would be necessary when people were tired. Lice Man would remind people that cleanliness was important. As for Old Age, without him there would never be enough room on Earth for new people.

Their mission accomplished, the world was now in peace and harmony – *hozho* – and the twins went to each of the four sacred mountains. The Sun came to them and to Changing Woman. He offered the goddess a place to live with him in the West. Changing Woman agreed, but only after the Sun understood that she must be surrounded by animals and must change with the seasons. She was Earth and he was Sky. As for the twins, they went to the joining of the rivers in San Juan Valley.

The mythic hero's search for the father is a metaphor for a culture's search for a lost aspect of its foundations and for the individual's search for identity. Since the mother's conception is miraculous, and she is reluctant to discuss the matter, the hero in the myth is left with a crucial missing element of identity and has

View of the Navajo Twin Rocks, Bluff, Utah.

Henry Peabody, photograph of Nampeyo (Hopi-Tewa pottery maker) with examples of her work, 1900, Hano, First Mesa, Hopi Reservation, Arizona.

a natural longing to fill that gap. Unless the gap is filled, the basis for creation is incomplete.

Another example of the search for the father motif is found in the strange myth of Waterpot Boy. A small group of Tewa Indians from north of Santa Fe fled during the pueblo revolts of the late seventeenth century and settled near the ancient ruins of Sikyati in the eastern part of land occupied by the Hopi tribe. Tewa Indians in the Hopi Reservation, Arizona, as in New Mexico, are famous for their pottery making. In New Mexico, Maria Martinez (1887–1980) was known for her black pots. In Hopi the most famous Tewa potter was Nampeyo (1859–1942), whose name means 'the snake that does not bite'. The Hopi-Tewa tell a pottery-based story of a boy hero whose goal was to find his father and so to establish a renewed culture of wholeness.

It seems that a woman living in Sikyati had a beautiful daughter who refused to marry. One day, while the woman was making pots, she asked her daughter to help her mix some clay. The daughter agreed and stamped up and down for some time on some clay she had placed on a flat rock. Somehow, a bit of the clay entered her as she stamped and, naturally, she became pregnant. This made the mother angry, and when the girl gave birth, the older woman immediately realized that the baby was not a regular child but, as you might expect, a water-pot baby. When the girl's father came home from hunting he was delighted to find that his daughter had given birth to a water-pot child. Twenty days later, Waterpot Boy had grown enough to play with the other children of the village. The children liked him, but his mother cried all the time because her son had no arms or legs – just a mouth into which she put food.

After some time had passed, Waterpot Boy asked his grandfather if he could hunt rabbits with him. But the grandfather said he couldn't – not without arms or legs. The boy pleaded so much that the grandfather agreed to take him hunting. Waterpot Boy rolled along next to his grandfather down under the mesa. Suddenly he spotted a rabbit and he rolled as fast as he could towards it. On the way he banged against a rock and broke apart, but out of the broken pieces a handsome boy arose. That day the boy killed many rabbits before he returned to his grandfather, who was hunting in another place. 'Who are you?' the old man asked. 'Have you seen a rolling water pot?' When the boy tried to explain who he was, his grandfather at first did not believe him. But finally he did, and the two went home together. When they got there, the boy's mother was angry, thinking her father had brought an unwanted suitor for her. But once her father explained the situation, the woman calmed down, and the boy went off with the other village boys.

One day the boy asked his mother who his father was. His mother said she didn't know. 'Well, I'm going to find him,' the boy said. 'But I've never been with a man,' the mother said, 'so there's no place to look.' 'Still,' said the boy, 'I'm going to find him; I think I know where he is.' So his mother packed him a lunch and he went away on his search. He came to a spring where an old man was standing. 'Where are you going?' the man asked the boy. 'I'm going to that spring to look for my father,' he said. 'You won't find him,' said the man. 'Oh yes I will,' the boy insisted. 'Well who is your father?' demanded the man. 'I think you are,' the boy answered. At first the man glared at the boy, trying to scare him. The boy kept insisting the man was his father until the man finally embraced him and took him over to the spring and then down into it. The man said he was Red Water Snake. In the spring the boy found all of his father's dead relatives. They recognized him and greeted him. He stayed one night in the spring and then went home to tell his mother what had happened.

Soon the boy's mother became sick and died. The boy went back to the spring, and there he found his mother with all the other relatives. His father said that he had made his mother die so that the boy would come back to the spring and they could all be there together.

Waterpot Boy's miraculous conception, like that of Kutoyis, marks him as a hero. And like the Blackfoot hero, his role is to renew creation. He brings harmony to the people by re-establishing the connection between his father and his mother, representing the ancestors and the living people.

Some heroic quests in Native American mythology are undertaken by individuals who are not indicated as mythological heroes by events like miraculous births or amazing childhood feats. In this Ojibwe myth a young man undertakes a vision quest expected of all boys of a certain age. For him and for the youths of many tribes, the vision quest involves fasting and isolation; it is a spiritual experience that will change a child into a productive adult member of his community. The Ojibwe myth, in short, is a metaphor for the meaning of the vision quest ritual, for the concept that even ordinary people possess the potential to be heroes.

When the boy, Wunzh, shows physical signs of manhood, his father builds him a simple lodge in the forest where he can undergo his vision quest. It is springtime, and as Wunzh walks in the woods near his lodge, he becomes more aware than usual of the plants coming back to life in the warming earth around him. He wonders about this whole process – how plants die and then come back, some with poisonous berries, some with berries that are true medicine. Perhaps, he wonders, the dreams caused by his fasting can explain these things. As the days pass, the lack of food makes Wunzh weak. All he can do is lie in his lodge praying for dreams or visions that will teach him something of use to his people, who are experiencing hard times.

One day a figure appears in the lodge dressed in rich yellow and green with beautiful golden feathers on his head. The figure explains that the Great Spirit had appreciated the boy's prayers for his people's needs rather than for himself. The strange figure says his prayers can be answered if Wunzh agrees to wrestle with him. Wunzh, exhausted and weak after the days of fasting, agrees. The two wrestle until Wunzh is unable to continue. The strange figure stops, says the boy has done well, and announces that he will be back the next day for more wrestling. When he arrives, Wunzh is even more exhausted than before, but somehow, the weaker he becomes, the more determined and courageous he is. The two fight long and hard and once again the visitor stops the match, saying he will be back. Wunzh is truly exhausted when his opponent arrives the next day, but after a while the visitor stops the fight, declaring Wunzh the victor. He tells the boy that the Great Spirit has been pleased with him and that if he follows certain instructions, his people will receive a great boon to revive the tribe.

The divine being says that the next day will be the seventh day of the vision quest, that the boy's father will bring food to give him strength. After that the visitor will come for one last time in which he and Wunzh will wrestle and Wunzh will win. Wunzh was to strip his opponent of his clothes, lay him on the ground, clear the ground of weeds, bury him, and return regularly to weed the area. 'After a time,' he says to Wunzh, 'something will happen that will change the lives of your people.' Wunzh does exactly as told, and near the end of the summer he comes to the burial spot to discover there a beautiful plant with long green leaves, a plume of gold at its top, and clusters of something yellow at its sides. Wunzh recognizes that this was his wrestling visitor and suddenly he knows his visitor's name: Mondawmin (the spirit of corn). He rushes to find his father and explains what he has seen and done during his vision quest. If the people treat the plant as he has been instructed, they will have a food which would provide them with new life.

A visitor to the Keres Pueblo of San Felipe, south of Santa Fe, on 2 February can witness another example of the hero as saviour. In this case the scene is, in effect, a ritual drama, ostensibly celebrating the Christian feast of Candelaria (Candlemas), marking the presentation of the young Jesus at the Temple and the purification of his mother. In fact, the ritual is a mystery play celebrating human courage and the productive relationship between humans and animals in the sacrificial act of the hunt. As such, the ritual takes the viewers and participants back to a period in mythological history when humans and animals were said to have communicated directly and interacted positively in the newly created world.

At dawn, a lone young woman appears in the pueblo plaza decorated with pine trees to represent the natural world. Her hair flows down her back from a headdress of feathers. She wears a white dress with a red sash around her waist and white moccasins lined with fur. It is she who with her purity and her endurance must represent a spiritual force strong enough to attract the animals, and especially the buffalo, to the village to be sacrificed. The maiden springs into action, climbing swiftly into the hills behind the plaza.

There she encounters the animals played by dancers with mysterious horned headdresses and in the case of one a huge buffalo head. The girl herds the animals and leads them into the village. Then, throughout the day – four times in the morning, four times in the afternoon – she dances with the giant buffalo in a scene reminiscent of a 'Beauty and the Beast' pantomime. The principals are accompanied by a chanting chorus and a drum. The maiden is fearless in her movements among the animals. She dances simply, her hands going up and down in movements mirroring her feet, which tap the earth in time with the drumming and chanting. Her dance partner, the buffalo, is naked to the waist, his body painted black. His movements are slow and lumbering. The other animals surround the principals. Also naked to the waist, and wearing elk, deer and antelope headdresses with appropriate antlers, they carry single sticks to use as their front feet in the dance. They also appear to use the sticks as phalli, sometimes pumping the earth rhythmically with their sticks. It is almost as if they are a fertility chorus encouraging the union of the maiden and the buffalo. In keeping with the fertility theme, clowns (*koshare*) appear between the dance sets and,

George Catlin, *Buffalo Dance, Mandan*, 1835–7, oil on canvas.

Korczak Ziolkowski,
Crazy Horse Memorial,
20th century, rock
sculpture, Black Hills,
South Dakota.

in the tradition of their trickster ancestors, indulge in what would normally be inappropriate sexual antics and verbal innuendoes.

Late in the afternoon, during the final dance set, the mood changes. The chanting and drumbeats become wild, the maiden is nowhere to be seen, and hunters appear to kill the animals. As they are shot, the animals leap into the air and then fall limply to the

Amos Bad Heart Bull (Oglala Lakota), *Custer Battle Field (Battle of the Little Bighorn),* late 19th century, pictograph.

earth. Men appear to carry the sacrificed animals to various houses on the plaza. Eventually the animals return, simply because the ritual is over or as resurrected spirits, ready to be sacrificed in future hunts.

Native American history has many actual heroes who gave their lives in the struggle to preserve Indian integrity. Some have achieved almost mythic status even among non-natives, who appreciate their bravery as underdog outlaws. Most American schoolchildren have heard of Crazy Horse, the Lakota Sioux warrior and leader in the alliance of Sioux, Chayenne and Arapaho who in 1876 defeated General Custer (Custer's Last Stand) at the Battle of Greasy Grass (Battle of the Little Bighorn). Crazy Horse had been inspired by another Sioux Plains hero, Chief Sitting Bull, who envisioned a recreated Indian nation. Geronimo, an Apache medicine man and warrior who held out against white dominance of Native Americans, is another such hero. These are figures who have been romanticized by American history textbooks but who, for Native Americans, are tragic heroes who struggled against an indomitable force to re-create their nations and preserve their values. The heroes were ultimately sacrificed on the altar of what the proponents of white American exceptionalism saw as progress. Crazy Horse and Sitting Bull died from u.s. military bullets. Geronimo died as a prisoner of war.

Native American Creation and the U.S. Today

On the morning of 29 December 1890, the reconstructed regiment of Custer's Last Stand attacked a group of Sioux camping at Wounded Knee Creek in the Pine Ridge Reservation in South Dakota. The Sioux were led by Chief Big Foot, who was lying in his tent dying of pneumonia. Some three hundred Sioux, including Big Foot, died in the battle and massacre that ensued, many of them women and children. This was, in effect, the last gasp of the Native American resistance to what had begun with the 'discovery' of America in 1492.

The situation of the Sioux, like that of indigenous peoples elsewhere in the ever-expanding United States, had become desperate. The buffalo herds on which they depended had been purposefully destroyed by the American army and by hunters who came west on the new railroad. It was Philip Sheridan, a Union general during the American Civil War, who implemented the plan of destroying buffalo to help force the Native Americans of the Great Plains to move to reservations. Sheridan praised the hunters and troops that killed the buffalo as, in effect, solving the 'Indian problem'. Attempting to regain something of their past glory and power, many Plains tribes had joined the mystical Ghost Dance movement based on a vision of a revitalized Native American culture. It was the white fear of this movement and the possibility of its leading to rebellion that led to the massacre at Wounded Knee.

David Francis Barry, portrait photograph of Sitting Bull and Buffalo Bill Cody during Buffalo Bill's Wild West Show in Montreal, 1885.

Etahdleuh Doanmoe
(Hunting Boy),
View of an Attack,
c. 1876, ledger
drawing depicting
one of several clashes
between Southern
Plains Indians and the
U.S. Army during the
Red River War in 1874.

The humiliation of Native Americans, especially of those like Sitting Bull and Geronimo, had begun before the tragedy of Wounded Knee. In 1885 Sitting Bull had been lured off the reservation to perform with 'Buffalo Bill' Cody in the latter's Wild West touring show. As for Geronimo, the American government made use of his 'Indian outlaw' fame by taking him out of prison for display at various fairs and other public functions. He walked in President Theodore Roosevelt's inaugural parade even though he was still a prisoner of war. This diminishing and sentimentalizing of Native Americans in the post-Civil War and post-Indian Wars period and beyond rested on a foundation of something much more serious. As Euro-American settlers gradually moved west from the original British colonies, Native Americans unwilling to give up their homelands and hunting grounds were treated as obstructions to progress. Even the most prestigious of the founding

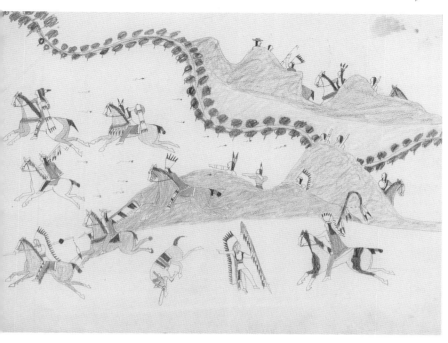

fathers subscribed to what was, in effect, a policy of 'necessary' genocide. George Washington advocated a policy that would treat Native Americans justly but as president also realized that American growth involved taking their lands. Thomas Jefferson during the whole of his political career spoke of the need to exterminate the natives or to move them further west, out of the way of the settlers. Benjamin Franklin wrote in his memoirs that the 'savages' stood in the way of the 'cultivators of the earth'. Later, under the Indian Wars 'hero' Andrew Jackson, native removal became policy in the Indian Removal Act of 1830.

One of the most notorious removals was that of the Cherokee, Choctaw, Chickasaw, Creek and Seminole – known as the Five Civilized Tribes – from the Southeast to what was then labelled 'Indian Territory' (now Oklahoma). The Trail of Tears, as it was called, involved the removal of native peoples who had essentially

Edward Bates, photograph of Apache Chief Geronimo telling his story to S. M. Barrett (left) and translator Asa Daklugie (right), *c.* 1905.

James A. West, *Points of View*, 2006, bronze, in Emerald View Park, Pittsburgh, depicting George Washington and Seneca Chief Guyasuta's face-to-face meeting in October 1770.

John Vanderlyn, *The Murder of Jane McCrea*, 1804, oil on canvas.

Alfred Boisseau,
*Louisiana Indians
Walking Along
a Bayou (The Trail
of Tears)*, 1848,
oil on canvas.

assimilated into the culture of the settlers, in terms of language, clothing, constitutional government and even religion. This removal and others, like the later forced Long Walk of the Navajo from their land to desolate Bosque Redondo, was part of the gradual marginalization of the tribes onto reservations. Furthermore, some five hundred treaties between the United States and the Native Americans had been signed beginning in 1778. Nearly all these treaties were violated by the government. Treaties, in fact, were a convenient means by which the European Americans in the eighteenth and nineteenth centuries, and even later, obtained native land. The Native American tribes never had a chance; they negotiated with the national government from a position of weakness because they were not a unified entity.

As settlers moved from east to west over what would become the United States, they confronted the Native Americans under what was, in effect, the banner of white supremacy. The 'only good Indian is a dead Indian' was a phrase in common usage. The Declaration of Independence, proclaiming that 'all men are created equal', had also mentioned 'the merciless Indian savages whose known rule of warfare, is undistinguished destruction of all ages, sexes and conditions'.

Deeply rooted in American history, then, is an essential conflict between the treatment of the Native Americans and the ideals of freedom and equality traditionally celebrated as the basis of American exceptionalism. The same conflict exists, of course, in connection with the Africans brought to America against their will to be enslaved.

American history from the *Mayflower* and Jamestown on, if viewed honestly, reveals that the United States of America rests on stolen land. For Americans, to deny that fact or to pretend ignorance of it is to deny ourselves, our own history. The Native American, like the African American, might well say, 'You can't have your history without me.' And once that history is recognized the whole idea of American exceptionalism, with its claims of liberty and equality for all, is called into question.

While it is unrealistic to suppose that this sore on the face of American history can be cured by the return of the stolen land, it is possible to face the reality of the false and ultimately genocidal mythology behind the settlement of what became the United States. In so doing, it is also possible to consider what might be learned from the worldview contained in the mythology of the dispossessed peoples.

Behind the genocide of the first Americans is a doctrine of exceptionalism and white supremacy, at the centre of which is the mythology of Manifest Destiny. 'Manifest Destiny' was a term coined in 1845 by a newspaper editor, John O'Sullivan, to put a label on an idea that attempted to justify the expansion of what became the United States into the lands populated by Native Americans who had been there for thousands of years. In fact, the concept of Manifest Destiny had existed since the arrival of the Pilgrims and the Jamestown settlers in the seventeenth century.

From the beginning, the invaders and settlers of North America from Europe believed that God had ordained that America be recreated as a 'New World' (as was also the case in Meso-America and South America), a new promised land, and that its original, heathen inhabitants be replaced through conversion or conquest by Christians who understood and appreciated the value of the land and its resources.

What the builders of the New World ignored or disparaged was the worldview and history of the people who already lived there before they arrived. The image of Squanto teaching the Pilgrims how to plant and fertilize corn is known to most Americans, but 'bad Indians' perched on hilltops in their war paint waiting to attack good settlers in their wagon trains quickly replaced Squanto in the national psyche.

John Gast, *American Progress*, 1872, oil on canvas.

Herbert W. Collingwood, 'Squanto (Tisquantum) Teaching the Plymouth Colonists How to Plant Corn with Fish', *c.* 1910, illustration in *Why the Fish Failed: A Story of Potash* (New York, n.d.).

The movement from Squanto to war and massacre hides a lost opportunity. Had the settlers really represented a search for a new world – one free of the inequities of the old world from which they had fled – they might have learned valuable alternatives from the people they dispossessed.

The essence of what is, in effect, a collective Native American worldview is evident in the four mythic personalities present in the creation myths discussed above: the Great Spirit, the trickster, the goddess and the hero. Although we European Americans have tended to equate the Great Spirit with our own monotheistic God, there is, in fact, a radical difference between the two views of deity and its function. Christians, like Jews and Muslims, worship a single entity – that is, God, Yahweh or Allah, respectively – who sits at the top of a hierarchical ladder on which humans and animals and plants rest on rungs below. The biblical concept of humans being placed in the world with the purpose of controlling all the other creatures and elements is a foreign idea to Native American mythology, at least before any conversions to the biblical view. Among traditional Native Americans there is no theology as such, no real worshipping of a deity. The Great Spirit is not a supreme god controlling all of creation, but a collective metaphor for the spiritual presence – the sacredness – of all of creation, a metaphor for an animistic under-standing of creation in which the spirit animates equally all aspects of life, plants, animals and people. In the animistic understanding, humans are not above all other creatures, as the Bible tells us we are. Rather, humans are a part of an intricate interrelated reality in which all aspects of the living world participate in the process of creation. It is not a supreme deity, but little animals who dive into the maternal waters to find the first soil in so many native earth-diver creation myths. In the Buffalo Dance ritual an unarmed human child ascends the mountain to find the buffalo who comes willingly into the village to be sacrificed for the good of all. And it is humans in consort with various creatures and elements of nature who must find their way out of the earth itself to be born into this world in the emergence myths of the American Southwest. This whole sense of the role of all of nature – including humans – in the continuing creation process results in a sense of the sacredness of this earth in the here and now.

In the context of today's world, the Great Spirit is a deeply eco-logical concept of which our world and we ourselves are aspects. The earth itself is sacred. To desecrate the land for profit or control is to desecrate the Great Spirit. As member elements of the Great Spirit, Americans would have to rethink ideas such as the 'conquest' of nature, the dominance of an all-powerful god, the supremacy of a race or the exceptionalism of a nation.

The central role of the trickster in Native American mythology is in keeping with an earth-centred rather than god-centred under-standing of creation. The trickster represents the unbridled energy in creation. He challenges the conventional; he is amoral and chaotic. The trickster epitomizes the appetites and drives within us that are difficult to control but which are in themselves necessary for life. He breaks all the appetite boundaries. In this sense he is like a child; he represents what we all are before we learn the rules of community. Like small children, Raven is fascinated by urine and faeces; when Coyote or Iktome want gratification of any kind, they spare nothing to satisfy their urges. In this the trickster also represents the difficulty we sometimes face in adhering to social rules and mores even after we have apparently grown up.

The trickster is one of our oldest mythological characters. Of all the characters in Native American myths, it is he who is closest to animals, representing a time when all aspects of the animistic world – of the Great Spirit – could communicate with each other. Thus it is that, as a transformer and shapeshifter, he can take human form or his animal form as Coyote, Raven, the Spider or the Hare. In his later incarnation as the shaman, he maintains the ability to move between worlds, keeping our contact with the spirits that animate the earth in which we live.

In fact, for the Native American the trickster has traditionally been an important bridge between the Great Spirit all around us and our created world. In the creation myths in which the process is initiated by the deity representing the Great Spirit, it is often the trickster who is at the creator's side and often the trickster who is left in the new world as a culture hero to teach the people how to reproduce, eat and order their lives. In this role the trickster also introduces the dark side of life. As a culture hero the Maidu Coyote, for instance, introduces death to his people. But, as we know, without death there could not be life; there could not be a continuing creation. In this sense, the trickster is the realist as opposed to the utopian vision of creation in Native American mythology.

The trickster is the figure in Native American mythology most foreign to European Americans and the Manifest Destiny mythology. He is the opposite of sentimentality and idealism. On one hand he represents creativity. On the other, to consider his meaning honestly is to accept the imperfection inherent in our collective life. In the context of the American experience, the trickster can represent our creativity and our belief in individualism. He can also help us, by extension, to confront the dark side of our history – the collective greed of Manifest Destiny and the collective hypocrisy of our sense of exceptionalism.

Like the trickster, the goddess plays a central role in Native American creation mythologies. She is of particular importance to the many matrilineal tribes, including, for instance, the Athabascans (Navajos and Apaches), the Iroquoians, the Cherokee, the Hopi and the Keresan-speaking Pueblos. But she also fills important roles in patrilineal tribes such as the Sioux and other Plains tribes.

The goddess as mother falls from the sky in eastern earth-diver myths. Her leaving the sky world of mysterious powers to form a world from dirt retrieved from the primordial maternal waters by humble animals establishes the centrality of earth rather than sky worship in the lives of her people. As the Corn Mother willingly sacrificed for the good of all in agricultural myths, she represents the importance of life cycles, including death in the Earth Mother. As White Buffalo Calf Woman, she, in effect, acts as a mystical culture hero bringing renewal to the people by way of new rites and mores. She and the Corn Mother emphasize that creation is a continuous phenomenon. And in the western emergence myth, the goddess is literally the Great Mother giving birth to the people from within herself. It is of interest that the emergence myth is honoured generally by most Native Americans because it stands as a metaphorical answer to the long unanswered question of non-Native American scholars: where did these peoples come from?

Whatever form she takes, the goddess is foreign to the highly patriarchal, monotheistic, land-ownership worldview of Manifest Destiny. The white settlers of North America had little experience of goddesses, and, unfortunately, their descendants have continued to take little notice of them. The goddess represents the sacredness of the earth itself and its gifts. If to desecrate the earth for profit or short-term convenience is to desecrate the Great Spirit, it is also to desecrate the earth as Mother.

The mythic hero is more familiar than the trickster or the goddess to European Americans. We know about the heroic labours of Herakles and St George's killing of the dragon. These heroes and others like them embody values such as bravery, perseverance, self-reliance and cultural pride. As a young country with a limited mythological base, the heroes associated with the United States, with the possible exception of Paul Bunyan, are primarily historical figures endowed with exaggerated powers. Daniel Boone's feats as a frontiersman reflect the American belief in the movement westward. The tall tales of the frontiersman and congressman Davy Crockett stand for the same belief. George Washington, who cut down the cherry tree and 'never told a lie', and Abe Lincoln, who grew up in a log cabin, speak to what the new American nation saw as its exceptional non-European honesty and egalitarianism.

The heroes who already existed on the American continent when the invaders and future settlers arrived represented somewhat different values and aspirations which would have been useful to the newcomers and might have tempered the effects of Manifest Destiny. As monster killers like Kutoyis and Glooscap and seekers like Waterpot Boy and Wunzh, their concern was with all the people. Community rather than individualism is celebrated in these hero myths. The historical heroes like Geronimo and Sitting Bull, too, were more concerned with saving their people than with individual honour. Sitting Bull saw in the Ghost Dance movement, for instance, a chance to recreate his people. In this hope he shared with Kutoyis and Waterpot Boy and with the trickster and the goddess the particular Native American understanding that creation is an ongoing process rather than something that occurred once, long ago.

The myth of Manifest Destiny, with its monotheistic and eventually nationalistic and consumeristic worldview, has had no place for Native Americans and their understanding of a continual and living creation in an animistic and polytheistic world. As a result, Native American myths – cultural dreams – as the reflection of a worldview, have been of little or no interest to Americans of the United States. American schoolchildren for the most part do not learn Native American myths and history. American society tends to find it simpler to treat Native Americans as a remnant of a sentimentally perceived past. The result has been a blindness among Americans to what should be an essential element of our existence in the place we have settled as our 'promised land'. By ignoring the Native American myths, and therefore failing to think through to the reality reflected in them, we lose a chance to embrace the soul of the land itself and so to work towards the overcoming of a significant element of our national racism and ideological hypocrisy.

Map of Native American Tribes

Overleaf:
William C. Sturtevant,
*Map of the Early
Indian Tribes, Culture
Areas, and Linguistic
Stocks*, 1967.

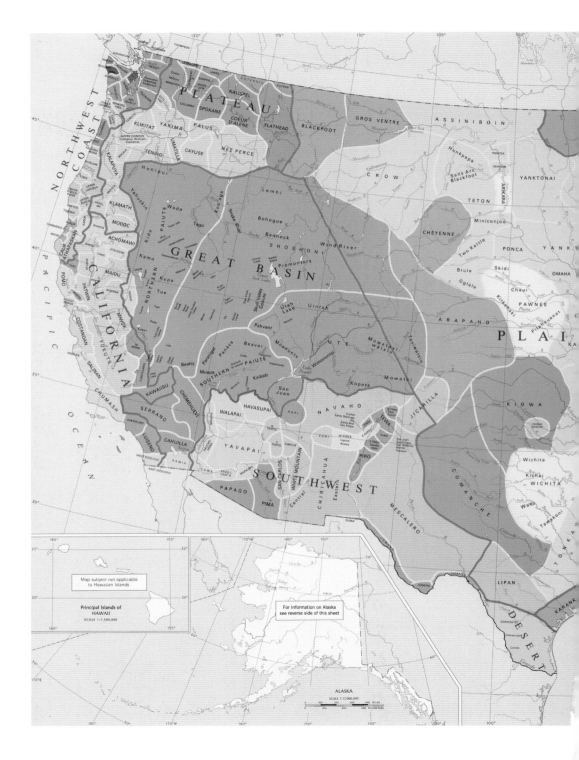

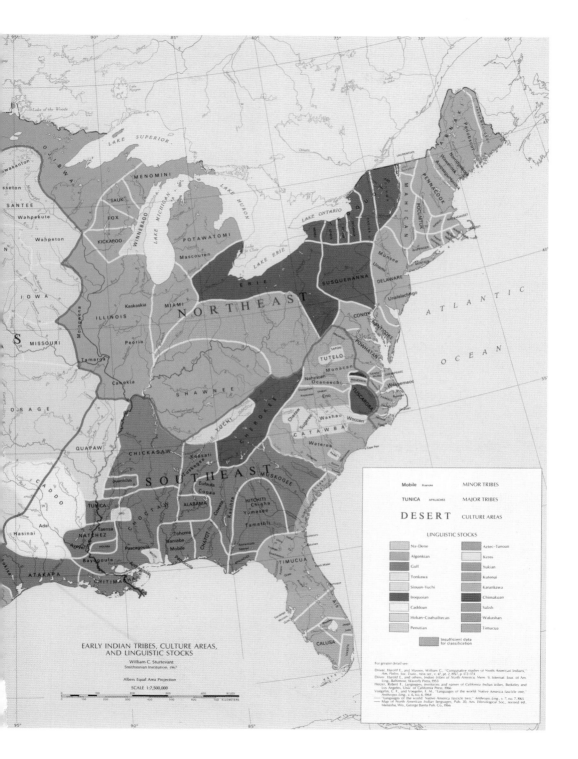

EARLY INDIAN TRIBES, CULTURE AREAS,
AND LINGUISTIC STOCKS

William C. Sturtevant
Smithsonian Institution, 1967

Albers Equal Area Projection

SCALE 1:7,500,000

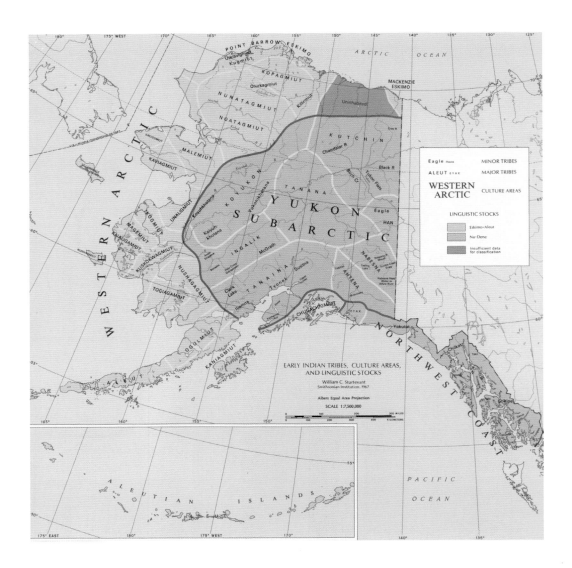

EARLY INDIAN TRIBES, CULTURE AREAS,
AND LINGUISTIC STOCKS

William C. Sturtevant
Smithsonian Institution, 1967

Albers Equal Area Projection

SCALE 1:7,500,000

Bibliography

Adovasio, J. M., with Jake Page, *The First Americans: In Pursuit of Archaeology's Greatest Mystery* (New York, 2002)

Alexander, Hartley Burr, *Native American Mythology*, revd edn (New York, 2005)

Allen, Paula Gunn, *Grandmothers of the Light: A Medicine Woman's Sourcebook* (Boston, MA, 1991)

Babcock, Barbara, 'A Tolerated Margin of Mess: The Trickster and His Tales Reconsidered', in *Critical Essays on Native American Literature*, ed. Andrew Wiget (Boston, MA, 1985)

Bastian, Dawn E., and Judy K. Mitchell, *Handbook of Native American Mythology* (Santa Barbara, CA, 2004)

Bierhorst, John, *The Mythology of North America* (New York, 1985)

Brown, Joseph Epes, ed., *The Sacred Pipe: Black Elk's Account of the Seven Rites of the Oglala Sioux* (Norman, OK, 1989)

—, *The Spiritual Legacy of the American Indian* (New York, 1989)

Champagne, Duane, ed., *Contemporary Native American Issues* (Walnut Creek, CA, 1999)

Clayton, Matt, *Native American Mythology* (Ormond Beach, FL, 2019)

Curtin, Jeremiah, *Native American Creation Myths* [1898] (New York, 2004)

Edmonds, Margot, and Ella E. Clark, *Voices of the Winds: Native American Legends* (New York, 1989)

Erdoes, Richard, and Alfonso Ortiz, *American Indian Myths and Legends* (New York, 1984)

Fergusson, Erna, *Dancing Gods: Indian Ceremonials of New Mexico and Arizona* (Albuquerque, NM, 1990)

Gill, Sam D., and Irene F. Sullivan, *Dictionary of Native American Mythology* (New York and Oxford, 1992)

Hultkrantz, Åke, *The Religions of the American Indian* (Berkeley, CA, 1981)

Kroeber, Karl, *Artistry in Native American Myths* (Lincoln, NE, 1998)

Lake-Thom, Bobby, *Spirits of the Earth: A Guide to Native American Nature Symbols, Stories, and Ceremonies* (New York, 1997)

Leeming, David A., *Creation Myths of the World* (Santa Barbara, CA, 2010)

—, and Jake Page, *The Mythology of Native North America* (Norman, OK, 1998)

Mann, Charles C., *1491: New Revelations of the Americas Before Columbus* (New York, 2011)

Martin, Joel W., *The Land Looks After Us: A History of Native American Religion* (Oxford and New York, 1999)

Miller, David Humphreys, *Custer's Fall: The Indian Side of the Story* (Lincoln, NE, 1957)

Mullett, G. M., *Spider Woman Stories: Legends of the Hopi Indians* (Albuquerque, NM, 1982)

Ostler, Jeffrey, *Surviving Genocide: Native Nations and the United States from the American Revolution to Bleeding Kansas* (New Haven, CT, and London, 2020)

Page, Jake, *In the Hands of the Great Spirit: The 20,000-year History of American Indians* (New York, 2003)

Radin, Paul, *The Trickster: A Study in American Indian Mythology* [1956] (New York, 2015)

Ramen, Fred, *Native American Mythology* (New York, 2008)

Saunt, Claudio, *Unworthy Republic: The Dispossession of Native Americans and the Road to Indian Territory* (New York, 2020)

Silverman, David, *This Land Is Their Land: The Wampanoag Indians, Plymouth Colony, and the Troubled History of Thanksgiving* (New York, 2019)

Spence, Louis, *The Myths of the North American Indians* [1914] (Toronto, 1989)

Tedlock, Dennis and Barbara, *Teachings from the American Earth* (New York, 1992)

Teuton, Sean, *Native American Literature: A Very Short Introduction* (Oxford and New York, 2018)

Thomas, R Murray., *Manitou and God: Indian Religions and Christian Culture* (Westport, CT, 2007)

Tyler, Hamilton A., *Pueblo Gods and Myths* (Norman, OK, 1964)

Vecsey, Christopher, ed., *Religion in Native North America* (Moscow, ID, 1990)

Weigle, Marta, *Creation and Procreation: Feminist Reflections on Cosmogony and Parturition* (Philadelphia, PA, 1989)
Wiget, Andrew, *Native American Literature* (Boston, MA, 1985)
—, ed., *Critical Essays on Native American Literature* (Boston, MA, 1985)
Williamson, Ray, *A Living Sky: The Cosmos of the American Indian* (Norman, OK, 1984)

Acknowledgements

I am grateful to the many people who, over the years, have provided me with direct and indirect contact with Native American cultures and myths. These include, among many others, Susanne Page, Dr John Talley, Professor Marta Weigle, and especially Jake Page and Little Antelope, to whose memory this book is dedicated.

Photo Acknowledgements

The author and publishers wish to express their thanks to the below sources of illustrative material and/or permission to reproduce it. Some locations of artworks are also given below, in the interest of brevity:

Adobe Stock/wxs2102: pp. 14–15; Autry Museum of the American West, Los Angeles, CA: p. 120; Boston Public Library, MA: p. 29; The British Museum, London: pp. 38, 85; Cleveland Museum of Art, OH: p. 88; from Edward S. Curtis, *Indian Days of Long Ago* (Yonkers, NY, 1915), photo Harold B. Lee Library, Brigham Young University, Provo, UT: p. 56; Denver Art Museum, CO: pp. 39, 80; photo Vit Ducken/Pixabay: pp. 78–9; photos Heritage Auctions, HA.com: pp. 114–15; from Antonio de Herrera y Tordesillas, *Historia General de las Indias Ocidentales, ò, De los hechos de los Castellanos en las Islas y Tierra firme del Mar Oceano*, vol. I (Antwerp, 1728): p. 12; photo Nick Kwan/Unsplash: p. 58; from Charles G. Leland, *The Algonquin Legends of New England* (London, 1884), photo University of Connecticut Library, Storrs: p. 92; Library of Congress, Geography and Map Division, Washington, DC: pp. 128–9, 130; Library of Congress, Prints and Photographs Division, Washington, DC: pp. 40, 41, 99, 112; Museum of Photographic Arts, San Diego: p. 73; National Archives at College Park, MD: pp. 82, 103; National Anthropological Archives, Smithsonian Institution, Washington, DC: pp. 30, 45, 75; National Gallery of Canada, Ottawa: p. 24; National Portrait Gallery, Smithsonian Institution, Washington, DC: p. 13; from *North American Indian Fairy Tales: Folklore and Legends* (London, 1905): p. 52; New Orleans Museum of Art, LA: p. 118; from *Old Indian Legends: Retold by Zitkála-Šá* (Boston, MA, 1901): p. 49; courtesy of the Oscar Howe Family and the University Of South Dakota Art Galleries, Vermillion: p. 86; courtesy Dr Mikkel Winther Pedersen: p. 20; from J. W. Powell (director), *Seventh Annual*

reasonable manner, but not in any way that suggests the licensor endorses you or your use.

share alike – If you remix, transform, or build upon the material, you must distribute your contributions under the same license as the original.

Index

Page numbers in *italics* refer to illustrations